BE the LEADER YOU WERE MEANT to BE

What the Bible Says about Leadership

LeRoy Eims

While this book is designed for the reader's personal use and profit, it is also intended for group study. A leader's guide with visual aids (Victor Multiuse Transparency Masters) is available from your local bookstore or from the publisher.

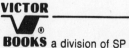

VICTOR

BOOKS a division of SP Publications, Inc.
WHEATON. ILLINOIS 60187

Offices also in
Whitby, Ontario, Canada
Amersham-on-the-Hill, Bucks, England

All Scripture quotations in this book are
from the King James Version.

Nineteenth printing, 1985

Library of Congress Catalog Card No. 75-5392
ISBN 0-88207-723-6

VICTOR BOOKS
A division of SP Publications, Inc.
            Wheaton, Ill. 60187

About the Author

LeRoy Eims is director of evangelism worldwide for The Navigators, an international organization training Christians to reproduce in others their life-changing relationships with Christ. He is much in demand as a conference speaker on evangelism and Christian leadership.

Eims' concern for some years has been the development of leaders committed to excellence—in their personal lives and as examples to those whom they lead. A combat marine in World War II, Eims has seen firsthand the results of excellent and poor leadership—in terms of human lives. In the arena of Christian warfare the best in leadership is demanded.

This book is an outgrowth of Eims' personal study of the Scriptures and his sharing of leadership principles with others. It is chock-full of biblical examples and personal experiences, an outgrowth of his ministry around the world.

He and his wife, Virginia, have three children, Larry and Becky, both in their 20s, and Randy, in his late teens.

To Mrs. Dawson Trotman,
woman of God,
spiritual mother to thousands
in every corner of the earth.

Contents

Foreword

For nearly two decades I have had the opportunity of observing LeRoy Eims in the role of a leader. I have seen him take young men who seem to be purposeless in life and patiently work with them to produce leaders. I've also seen his leadership in directing training centers to prepare college students for effective Christian service and leadership. Being strong in self-discipline, he has instilled in many of them a truly disciplined life.

Mr. Eims is a good Bible student and has based the contents of this book on sound biblical principles. By precept, he first shows God's methods of leadership. Then he illustrates these precepts by biblical examples as well as by many personal experiences. In other words, he's not teaching idealism but principles of leadership based on the Bible and experienced in personal life.

It will be well for Christian workers and leaders to read and reread this book and to put into practice these proven, basic principles of spiritual leadership. I also believe this book can serve well as a guide for leaders to use in training others.

I thus highly recommend this book to believers everywhere.

THEODORE H. EPP,
Founder and Director
Back to the Bible Broadcast

Preface

A crisis of leadership engulfs the world. Political leaders, economic experts, editorial writers, newsmen, spokesmen in the fields of education and religion raise the hue and cry: men who know the way and can lead others on the right path are few.

Leadership comes in all varieties. Good and bad. Effective and ineffective. Positive and negative. Right and wrong.

We need to look at leadership from the standpoint of the Bible. Both Old and New Testaments are alive with eternal truths that bear on this subject. The teachings of Christ Himself burst forth in clear and understandable principles. To analyze and apply these biblical teachings is my aim.

This book goes forth with the prayer that God will use it to increase the ranks of men and women who will provide leadership true to the Word of God, faithful to Jesus Christ, and committed to the work and will of God.

LeRoy Eims

1

Who Is Fit
to Lead?

Before a person takes on a leadership responsibility, he should weigh the matter carefully. "My brethren, be not many masters, knowing that we shall receive the greater condemnation" (James 3:1). The leader will be held in more severe and stricter judgment than his followers. That one thought should give us pause.

The next sentence in that same chapter gives another reason: "For in many things we offend all." We know ourselves and know that we make many a slip; we stumble in so many ways. That being the case, we are naturally hesitant to presume to lead others.

However, it is abundantly evident in analyzing the lives of God's great leaders that this feeling of inadequacy is not a good reason for declining the job. After all, we are all sinners before God. Who among us could claim that we have not blown it in many ways and in many different situations? If that is an adequate reason for not stepping up and taking the lead, no one would ever do so.

Let's look at some of God's chosen leaders of the past and see how they responded when the Lord approached them to take the lead in a task.

The Call of Moses
Take a look at Moses. He was in the backside of the desert keeping the flock of Jethro his father-in-law when God's call came. The very fact that this highly educated man, who had been accustomed to the comforts and pleasures of the palace, was occupied in one of the lowliest pursuits of his day could have been enough to em-

bitter him. Herding sheep was a profession held in low esteem. He could have been moping around feeling sorry for himself, so occupied with his misery and ill fortune as to miss the voice of God completely. To top it off, he was working for his in-laws!

Then a strange and wonderful thing happened. "And the angel of the Lord appeared unto him in a flame of fire out of the midst of a bush: and he looked, and, behold, the bush burned with fire, and the bush was not consumed" (Ex. 3:2).

The first thing the Lord did was reveal Himself to Moses. Moses was certain that it was God who spoke to him (see vv. 5-6). This is something that you must be sure about in your own mind. When someone comes to ask you to serve in one way or another, make certain that God is in it. Don't budge an inch in either direction—either yes or no—until you have determined the will of God in the matter.

Sometimes you will know God's will immediately. Other times you will have to wait until God makes it plain to you. But be assured of this—God will show you. Our Father in heaven is well able to communicate to His children. God will confirm His will in the matter to you. He does not want us to spend our lives in uncertainty.

Since God is concerned with what we do, He will make His will known. He promises to do so. "I will instruct thee and teach thee in the way which thou shalt go: I will guide thee with Mine eye" (Ps. 32:8). In this verse, notice the pronoun *I*, referring to God, appears twice. Guidance is God's responsibility. The assurance of guidance is as basic in Scripture as is the assurance of forgiveness. Notice also God says, "I *will* instruct. I *will* teach. I *will* guide." He will show us the way to go. Blessed assurance!

Another promise is found in Psalm 48:14: "For this God is our God for ever and ever: He will be our guide even unto death." The words of this promise are unmistakable: "He will be our guide." So you can rely on His willingness and ability to show you what His will is for you. Like Moses, you can be certain that God has spoken.

The next thing that occurred was that the Lord revealed to Moses the burden that He had for His people. "And the Lord said, 'I have surely seen the affliction of My people which are in Egypt, and have heard their cry by reason of their taskmasters; for I know their sorrows' " (Ex. 3:7). Moses, you recall, had been burdened over the plight of the children of Israel, and it was an encouragement for him to realize that God Himself was concerned for them as well.

Then God made a dramatic statement: "I am come down to deliver them out of the hand of the Egyptians, and to bring them up out of that land unto a good land and a large, unto a land flowing with milk and honey" (Ex. 3:8). Can you imagine the joy and excitement that must have flooded Moses' mind at that point? The living God was going to personally take a hand and deliver the people!

Then the Lord made a statement that must have thrown Moses into confusion. "Come now, therefore, and I will send thee unto Pharaoh, that thou mayest bring forth My people the children of Israel out of Egypt" (Ex. 3:10). Can't you just hear the questions flooding Moses' mind? "But Lord, I thought You said *You* were going to come down and deliver them. Why then this idea that I should go to Pharaoh and that *I* should bring forth the children of Israel out of Egypt? If You are going to do it, Lord, why do *I* need to go?"

That, by the way, is a key question each of us must get answered in his own mind. When we understand that God's *method* of accomplishing His plan and purposes is *people,* we will begin to understand our role in the kingdom of God.

So it was with Moses. God had a job for him. However, Moses did not feel qualified for the task that God had given him. And he cried out to God with his question, "Who am I?"

Now frankly, that is not all that hard of a question for God. He could have simply answered, "Thou art Moses." But the question was so irrelevant that God did not even bother to answer it.

Therein lies one of the great secrets of leadership in the Christian enterprise. God said, "Certainly I will be with thee." What the Lord was trying to get across to Moses was a powerful truth. He as much as said, "Moses, it doesn't really matter who you are—whether you feel qualified or unqualified, whether you feel up to the task or not. The point is that *I* am going to be there. The statement I made to you still holds: 'I am come down to deliver them.' I am going to do it, and I am going to give you the privilege of being in it with Me. You will be My instrument of deliverance."

By all means, remember this truth when you are called of God to take a position of leadership in His work. God is not looking for people who feel "sufficient." Paul said, "Not that we are sufficient of ourselves to think anything as of ourselves, but our sufficiency is of God" (2 Cor. 3:5).

I'm sure the sense of need and inadequacy can be an asset rather than a handicap. Paul's testimony bears this out: "And He said unto me, 'My grace is sufficient for thee: for My strength is made perfect in weakness.' Most gladly therefore will I rather glory in my infirmities, that the power of Christ may rest upon me. . . . For when I am weak, then am I strong" (2 Cor. 12:9-10).

Many people are amazed at that and say, "Do you mean the great Apostle Paul felt that way?" The answer is yes, and that no doubt contributed to his greatness.

The next lesson we learn in our look at the call of Moses is an important one as well. It is right to be aware of our inadequacy, but we mustn't stop there. We must also be convinced of the absolute sufficiency of God. That's God's next step in dealing with Moses.

Moses comes up with another question: "Behold, when I come unto the children of Israel and shall say unto them, 'The God of your fathers hath sent me unto you': and they shall say to me, 'What is His name?' what shall I say unto them?" (Ex. 3:13)

To this God gives a remarkable answer: "And God said unto Moses, 'I AM THAT I AM': and He said, 'Thus shalt thou say unto the children of Israel, "I AM hath sent me unto you." ' And God said moreover unto Moses, 'Thus shalt thou say unto the children of Israel, "The Lord God of your fathers, the God of Abraham the God of Isaac, and the God of Jacob, hath sent me unto you": this is My name for ever, and this is My memorial unto all generations' " (Ex. 3:14-15).

As a young Christian I puzzled over that answer for a long time. What did God mean when He revealed Himself as "I AM"? Then one day it hit me. God is saying, "Whatever you need, that's what I am!"

At this point in His life, Moses needed encouragement and strength. Quite possibly that will be your need when you receive your call from God to serve Him in some specific task.

More important, the fact that we are never without needs brings this truth into focus. Do we need comfort? *I am* your comfort: "Casting all your care upon Him, for He careth for you" (1 Peter 5:7). Do we need victory over some sin that plagues us? *I am* your victory. "But thanks be to God, which giveth us the victory through our Lord Jesus Christ" (1 Cor. 15:57). Do we need love? "God is love" (1 John 4:8). And so on down the catalogue of needs. God is absolutely sufficient to meet them. What God was saying was, *I am all that My people need.*

So it's true that we must acknowledge our insufficiency, but it must not stop there. If it does we are in trouble. We must go on to acknowledge the absolute adequacy and sufficiency of God to meet any test, to overcome any problem, and to win any victory. It took Moses a little time, but he did come to that point and was mightily used of God.

The Call of Gideon

To reinforce in our minds this absolutely essential truth of God's sufficiency, let's consider another man at the point of his call from God. Remember the great battles that were waged and won by Gideon? With a handful of men he "turned to flight the armies of the aliens." Was he always like that? Bold, courageous, waxing valiant in a fight?

Hardly!

The children of Israel were suffering under the hand of the Midianites. They were hiding in dens and caves in the mountains. The Midianites destroyed their crops and confiscated their live-stock. These enemies, like a plague of grasshoppers, consumed everything as they moved across the land. The reason for Israel's dilemma was, of course, their sin. "And the children of Israel did evil in the sight of the Lord: and the Lord delivered them into the hand of Midian seven years" (Jud. 6:1).

One night Gideon was threshing a little wheat to hide it from the Midianites. The angel of the Lord appeared and called upon him to be the instrument to deliver God's people out of the hand of the Midianites.

Gideon's first response was quite familiar to God by this time. "Oh my Lord, wherewith shall I save Israel? behold, my family is poor in Manasseh, and I am the least in my father's house' (Jud. 6:15).

Again, God went to the heart of the matter with His chosen man for the job. "Surely I will be with thee, and thou shalt smite the Midianites as one man" (Jud. 6:16).

Notice the similarity to what God told Moses at the burning bush. In effect, God said, "Gideon, it doesn't matter that your fam-ily is poor in Manasseh, or that you are least in your father's house. The point is not who you are, but that *I* will be with you. It is not your weakness that we must dwell on, but My strength. I will work through you."

So, if God calls you to a task and you have an overpowering sense of weakness and need and inadequacy—rejoice! You are in good company. Men of God down through the centuries have felt the same way. But they have also believed God to be sufficient for the task to which He has called them.

The Call of Jeremiah

There is one more person we must look at to round out this matter. Jeremiah was one of the great prophets of God. He was faithful to God's call and suffered for that faithfulness. But how did the call come? And how did Jeremiah respond when God spoke to him about assuming a position of leadership in His kingdom? Look at the record. "Then the word of the Lord came unto me, saying, 'Before I formed thee in the belly I knew thee; and before thou camest forth out of the womb I sanctified thee, and I ordained thee a prophet unto the nations' " (Jer. 1:4-5).

The basic job of a prophet was to proclaim the Word of God to the people of God. How did Jeremiah respond to this challenge? Did he immediately rise to the occasion with faith and enthusiasm? No, his response was similar to those of Moses and Gideon: "Then said I, 'Ah, Lord God! behold, I cannot speak: for I am a child' " (Jer. 1:6). His initial reaction was one of inadequacy. He didn't feel equal to the task.

Here's God's answer to that: "Say not, 'I am a child,' for thou shalt go to all that I shall send thee, and whatsoever I command thee thou shalt speak. Be not afraid of their faces: for *I* am with thee to deliver thee" (Jer. 1:7-8). Notice the promise of God: "I am with thee." Again, the point is that God is there. The all-wise, all-powerful, all-sufficient God will be by his side. In every case, this is the thing God keeps saying.

In the case of Jeremiah, God did not promise him a rose garden, but the assurance of His presence and protection and guidance was given time and again: " 'And they shall fight against thee; but they shall not prevail against thee; for I am with thee,' saith the Lord, 'to deliver thee' " (Jer. 1:19; see also 15:20; 20:11).

Other Calls—Then and Now

Do you recall the last orders of the Lord Jesus Christ to His followers? "Go and make disciples of all nations." Accompanying that charge to them was the promise, "I will be with you always" (Matt. 28:19-20, *New International Version*). God is still giving us the same basis for serving Him with confidence that He gave to old time heroes of the faith: *I am with you.*

Some years ago I was asked to speak at a Sunday School class retreat. For years Jim Rayburn, founder of the Young Life movement, had been teacher of the Mr. and Mrs. Class at First Presbyterian Church of Colorado Springs. The class was having its annual retreat, and they called on The Navigators for a speaker. Rod Sargent, to whom the request had first come, was unable to go, so he called me into his office and suggested I do it.

I froze. For a class taught by Jim Rayburn? What had I to offer to a class that had this man of God for a regular teacher? "Behold I cannot speak," I thought to myself, "for I am a child." I was only about six or seven years old in the Lord at the time, and most of the people there would be my elders both physically and spiritually. So I began to explain this all to Rod and asked him to get someone else.

Rod sat there looking at me and didn't say anything for quite a while. Then he spoke. "LeRoy," he said, "one thing I've noticed about you. You always seem to want to take the course of least resistance. You shy away from something that may be difficult or require a real step of faith." Then he told me to think about it for awhile and pray about it.

I did. Though I *still* felt inadequate for the task, the Lord definitely spoke to me about accepting it. Needless to say, I prepared with much study and hours of prayer.

To my delight the retreat went quite well. I sensed the presence and guidance of God and His enabling power. The Lord taught me some very helpful lessons through that situation—not the least of which was the truth of God's admonition that I must not move through life taking the course of least resistance. The experience was good for me; hard, but valuable down through the years.

Another thing the devil may use to prevent us from stepping out by faith in response to the call of God is something undesirable in our background. We may feel this disadvantage is too much to overcome or that it will be a hindrance to the work. Again, the Scriptures remind us of the fallacy of this argument.

The Apostle Paul, you recall, was a murderer who had spent a great deal of time and energy persecuting the church of God. He later confessed with shame: "I imprisoned and beat in every synagogue them that believed on Thee; And when the blood of Thy martyr Stephen was shed, I also was standing by, and consenting unto his death, and kept the raiment of them that slew him" (Acts 22:19-20).

Paul described himself as "not meet to be called an apostle, because I persecuted the church of God" (1 Cor. 15:9). But he also wrote, "I thank Jesus Christ our Lord, who hath enabled me, for that He counted me faithful, putting me into the ministry, who was before a blasphemer, and a persecutor, and injurious" (1 Tim. 1:12-13).

If ever a man had a background that would render him unusable to God, it was Paul. Yet he became the great apostle to the Gentiles and was used of God to write much of the New Testament.

Other people with dark blots on their records became great servants of God as well. I think of John Mark, the man who proved to be an unfaithful servant on a journey with Paul and Barnabas. When these men planned their next journey, Paul refused to take Mark along because of his past failure (see Acts 15:36-38).

Yet this is the man whom God chose to write the Gospel of Mark, which presents His own Son as the ever faithful servant. Mark's background was certainly not the thing that was the basis for God's choosing him for the task.

David was chosen by God to be the commander and leader of His people and to be administrative head of the government. His background was that of a shepherd tending the sheep on the rolling hills of the land of Israel. But God called him and he followed. His background, or lack of it, was not an issue.

So when God calls you to a task let neither a sense of inadequacy or a "poor background" hinder you from following His lead. "For it is God which worketh in you, both to will and to do of His good pleasure" (Phil. 2:13).

2

The Leader's
Source of Power

A power failure can be disastrous. Hospitals and other vital facilities have their backup systems of generators in case the power fails. This equipment must keep functioning because lives depend on it. Power and the means to use it are critical to an industrialized society.

Today the fuel shortage is felt around the world. People drive slower, thermostats are set lower in winter and higher in summer than previously, and rows of Jumbo Jet 747s are parked in the desert, unused because of reduced airline schedules due to the high cost of aviation fuel. These huge wonders of the space age, built to span continents and oceans in hours, are stalled. When the source of power dries up, the machinery dependent on that power grinds to a halt.

The leader must be acutely aware of this. He has to realize that he must keep his program, his people, and himself moving. What is the leader's source of power for all this? God Himself.

Fellowship
The Apostle Paul said to one of his supporting churches, "I can do all things through Christ which strengtheneth me" (Phil. 4:13). David centuries earlier said, "God is my strength and power: and He maketh my way perfect" (2 Sam. 22:33). God Himself is our source of power, but *fellowship* with God is that which "throws the switch," and makes that power operative and effective in our lives. The greatest preparation for David's leadership as king

was his time spent alone with God as a shepherd boy in the Judean hills.

Years alone *with* God prepared David for leadership *under* God. He certainly saw leadership in operation firsthand while living in the palace as a youth, but his time with God was of greater value to him than his time with men. As the leader of his army and administrator of the nation, he had little preparation from the human point of view. He had no courses in ROTC. He did not take Business Administration 101, but he knew God.

This area, also, is where the devil strikes the hardest. He may take mild interest in your attendance at leadership seminars or in your subscription to *Business Week*. But when you get serious about knowing God through vital fellowship with Him, he mounts an all-out attack to prevent it. You will find your schedule disrupted and many urgent matters to consider. You will be much too busy to fellowship with the Lord.

Why does the enemy of our souls fight time with God so furiously? Because of its imperative nature in the life of the leader. What are the spiritual rewards that come our way, we might ask, if we are faithful to our fellowship with God? To answer that question we must ask another. What is man's ultimate purpose on earth? The answer: "Even every one that is called by My name: for I have created him for My glory, I have formed him; yea, I have made him" (Isa. 43:7). "Man's chief end is to glorify God and to enjoy Him forever." Often people recite that statement of the Westminster Shorter Catechism but they really don't know what it means in daily life.

I recall discussing that with a group of seminary students. They knew that our purpose for being on earth was to glorify God. I asked one of them what a person did to accomplish that. How *do* you glorify God? His face took on a quizzical look and with a grin that was prompted more by shame than humor he said, "I haven't the faintest idea." Imagine that! Here was a group of men preparing for spiritual leadership and they had no idea of how to accomplish their primary goal in life.

Let me share with you a simple lesson I learned as a young Christian. God originally created man to glorify His name. He created man in His own image for fellowship with Himself. God had a close relationship with man in the garden. But then man sinned. He disobeyed God. He brought dishonor to His name. The image was marred and the fellowship broken. When the time was just right, however, God took a decisive step to recreate man's potential to bring glory to His name.

Was there ever a man whose every thought, word, and deed brought glory to God every hour of every day of every year of his life? Yes. One. The Lord Jesus Christ. In Jesus' prayer to His Father, He said of Himself, "I have glorified Thee on the earth: I have finished the work which Thou gavest Me to do" (John 17:4). Therefore, if I am ever to accomplish my ultimate goal in life, to glorify God, I must be transformed more and more into His image, to become like Christ.

The desire of God's heart is for us to become like His Son. "For whom He did foreknow, He also did predestinate to be conformed to the image of His Son, that He might be the firstborn among many brethren" (Rom. 8:29). This glorifies God.

How then do I become like Christ? How does my person become like another? By being around the person, talking with him, doing things together. Have you ever seen a picture of a couple who have lived together for 50 years and are celebrating their golden wedding anniversary? They not only act alike and enjoy the same things and have the same tastes; they even look alike!

I remember the day when Lt. Al Vail of the U.S. Marine Corps married Margie Igo, a charming, beautiful, intelligent graduate of Stanford. They had met at a Christian conference in Colorado, and Al fell head over heels in love with Margie. In typical Marine fashion he launched a campaign to win this fair young maiden. Letters, phone calls, flowers, and gifts began to arrive.

At first Margie was a bit startled by it all, but after some months the Lord confirmed in her heart that Al was God's choice for her, so they were married. A little over a year after the wedding I visited them in their home in Virginia.

When I arrived Margie apologized because I had to wait a few minutes for her to prepare my room. In her words, the room was not "squared away" yet.

"Squared away!" I thought. Stanford grads don't go about squaring things away. But this Stanford grad did because she had lived for a year with Lt. Al Vail, USMC, who made it his business to see that everything and everyone around him was "squared away." She had begun to pick up his mannerisms. Then Al came home, and I was startled to see how Margie's life had also affected him. They had lived together in fellowship with each other and were becoming like each other.

So it is with us in our relationship with the Lord. For us to be "conformed to the image of Jesus Christ" we must invest much time alone with Him in personal fellowship. The leader who will do this, who has a "built-in" devotional life rather than one that is "tacked on," will find himself in vital touch with God and being mightily used of God. God searches for such men. "And I sought for a man among them, that should make up the hedge, and stand in the gap before Me for the land, that I should not destroy it: but I found none" (Ezek. 22:30). This hunt is as new as our unborn sons and as old as the dawn of man. When God finds a person who will place as his first priority a life of intimate, personal, dynamic fellowship with Him, He directs His power, guidance, and wisdom into and through that person. God has found a man through whom He can change the world.

The Word of God
Three basic elements characterize a life of fellowship with the Lord. God speaks to us by means of His Word. "All Scripture is given by inspiration of God, and is profitable for doctrine, for reproof, for correction, for instruction in righteousness: that the man of God may be perfect, throughly furnished unto all good works" (2 Tim. 3:16-17).

We must get into the Word and the Word must get into us. We get into the World by hearing it preached, reading it, studying it, and memorizing it. We get the Word into us through meditation. By meditating on it we assimilate the Word of God into our spiritual lives. Like physical food, it is not what we take in that affects us but what we digest and assimilate. That's meditation. To meditate is to go deeply into the Word, to revolve it in our minds, to go below the surface. "O how love I Thy law! it is my meditation all the day" (Ps. 119:97).

In 1963 I visited London on a preaching tour. The schedule allowed us a day of sightseeing. David Limebear, a young man on our university team there, was assigned to be our tour guide and was eager to show us the sights and sounds of his beloved city. David arrived early in the morning armed with a list of historic places and the subway schedule. He had it all figured out, exactly when the underground railway would arrive at each point, how much time we had there, and when we had to leave to catch the next train for the next stop.

I entered into this sightseeing with the sort of excitement you'd expect to find in a boy from Neola, Iowa, about to see the big city. David was the athletic type, in top physical shape and he kept us on the move. We jogged through the cathedrals, sprinted through the parks, paused momentarily to gaze at the statues, and cast hasty glances at buildings that oozed grandeur and history. We really saw London—but did we?

Some years later my wife and I were there on another preaching assignment and our last day was spent with some people seeing the sights. The pace was leisurely. I saw and absorbed the beauty and majesty of the cathedrals I had jogged through some years before. This time my spirits were affected. I had time to really see them, to experience them, to sense the meaning and the message in them.

So it is with the Word of God. If we hurry through an assigned Bible reading, if we quickly grind out a Bible study for our group in a Sunday School class, if we're looking at our watch hoping the service will end so we can run to something else, little will happen in our lives. It's like jogging through a cathedral. We see it, but we don't really. But if we open the Word and take time to let the Spirit of God affect our lives, to absorb it into our souls, to see its beauty and grandeur, we will be in true fellowship with God.

God wants to communicate with us through His Word. If we take time to meditate, we will experience the depth and the greatness of the message, and the Spirit of God will speak to us and affect our lives. And here's an important point. It is God who does it, not the words printed on paper. God uses His Word as a means, as an instrument to communicate Himself to us. "My soul cleaveth unto the dust; quicken Thou me according to Thy Word" (Ps. 119:25). Note that it was God Himself who could breathe new life into the psalmist. He used His Word as an instrument to do it.

We need to develop a love for the Word of God. "O how love I Thy law! it is my meditation all the day" (Ps. 119:97). It was love for the Word of God that prompted the psalmist's meditation on the Word. That's the place to start. Ask God to give you a love for and delight in His Word. "Make me to go in the path of Thy commandments; for therein do I delight" (Ps. 119:35). "Praise ye the Lord. Blessed is the man that feareth the Lord, that delighteth greatly in His commandments" (Ps. 112:1). "And I will delight myself in Thy commandments, which I have loved" (Ps. 119:47).

The leader who is worth his salt and who will truly lead others spiritually must be a man of the Word.

Prayer

The second element of fellowship is prayer. God speaks to us through His Word and we speak to Him through prayer. The thing to remember is that there are prayers that move the hand of God and there are prayers that have no effect at all. What's the difference?

Jesus talked about the different kinds of praying in a parable. "Two men went up into the temple to pray; the one a Pharisee, and the other a publican. The Pharisee stood and prayed thus with himself, 'God, I thank Thee, that I am not as other men are, extortioners, unjust, adulterers, or even as this publican. I fast twice in the week, I give tithes of all that I possess.' And the publican, standing afar off, would not lift up so much as his eyes into heaven, but smote upon his breast, saying, 'God be merciful to me a sinner.' I tell you, this man went down to his house justified rather than the other: for every one that exalteth himself shall be abased; and he that humbleth himself shall be exalted" (Luke 18:10-14).

One summer I had the privilege of hearing a concert on the Potomac River in Washington, D.C. The orchestra was performing the *1812 Overture*. At one point in it there is cannon fire. The cannon don't try to hit anything; they just "fire for effect." It adds drama and excitement to the overture.

By way of contrast, I recall my days in the Marine Corps during World War II as a forward observer in an artillery unit. One of the pieces would fire a round and I would observe where it landed in relationship to the target. I would then radio a message to raise or lower, go right or left. They would fire another round and I would give new instructions. Finally, I would give the final instruction and call on them to "fire for effect."

I used the same expression as that relating to the overture, but meant something far different. At that point the entire battery would open up on the target, with devastating effect.

So it is in the parable of Jesus. The Pharisee was merely praying for effect, as a means to impress, and Jesus said, "He prayed thus with himself." The publican, on the other hand, did business with God. He prayed for effect, to accomplish something. This is the kind of prayer we should offer to God. "The effectual fervent prayer of a righteous man availeth much" (James 5:16). For a prayer to be effectual, it must be fervent.

This is illustrated by an incident in the Early Church (Acts 12:1-12). King Herod had begun a reign of terror and persecution against Christians. He had killed James, the brother of John, and was about to kill Peter also. Peter was in prison securely guarded by 16 soldiers. But prayer was made for him by the Christians and in response to that prayer the Lord sent an angel to release him.

Various translations use different words to describe the kind of prayer that was offered: earnest, fervent. The word that is used to describe the prayer is the word that is used to describe the intensity of feeling one has when being pulled apart on a torture rack.

The reason for this fervent prayer is obvious. First, it was physically impossible for Peter to escape. The main thing that prompted their fervent prayer, however, was Peter's past. He was known to have denied the Lord when the going got rough. Was God answering their prayers? Abundantly! The night before his execution Peter was sleeping like a baby, chained between two soldiers. The effectual fervent prayer of this little band of Christians availed much. Not only had Peter not defected, but he was released from prison in a most remarkable way. God heard and answered.

I made a house call with a doctor a few years ago. When the doctor completed his examination he said, "The man has a bad heart." I asked myself, how did he know. The man could have said that he never felt better, the old ticker was in good shape, and the doctor was wasting his time talking to him about it. But no matter what the man might have said, Dr. Frank knew he had a bad heart. How? Simple. He listened to the man's heart with a stethoscope and paid no attention to what the man was saying.

So it is with God. We don't pray into a spiritual microphone with God listening on a set of heavenly earphones. He listens to us pray with a spiritual stethoscope. "This people draweth nigh unto me with their mouth, and honoreth Me with their lips; but their heart is far from Me" (Matt. 15:8). Jeremiah's call to "pour out *thine* heart like water before the face of the Lord" (Lam. 2:19) must be heeded today.

Have you ever heard Christians say when they part, "I'll be praying for you." Great, if they would do it. But often it is merely a way of saying good-bye. How different were the words of the

Apostle Paul, "For God is my witness, whom I serve with my spirit in the Gospel of His Son, that without ceasing I make mention of you always in my prayers" (Rom. 1:9).

For prayer to be fervent it must be specific. Too often we fall into the rut of praying, "God bless the church," or "God encourage the missionaries," or "God help the class." The leader's praying must be specific in two areas.

First, the leader's prayers should concentrate on the growth and development of each of the people whom he leads. The Apostle Paul gave us an example: "For this cause we also, since the day we heard it, do not cease to pray for you, and to desire that ye might be filled with the knowledge of His will in all wisdom and spiritual understanding: that ye might walk worthy of the Lord unto all pleasing, being fruitful in every good work and increasing in the knowledge of God" (Col. 1:9-10). Likewise, consider the prayers of Epaphras. "Epaphras, who is one of you, a servant of Christ, saluteth you, always laboring fervently for you in prayers, that ye may stand perfect and complete in all the will of God" (Col. 4:12). Second, the leader should pray for the spiritual maturity of his people and that God might raise up from their midst laborers to go into the harvest fields of the world.

Jesus Himself instructs us to do this. "When He saw the multitudes, He was moved with compassion on them, because they fainted, and were scattered abroad, as sheep having no shepherd. Then saith He unto His disciples, 'The harvest truly is plenteous, but the laborers are few; pray ye therefore the Lord of the harvest, that He will send forth laborers into His harvest'" (Matt. 9: 36-38).

Obedience

The last element of fellowship is obedience. There is no fellowship with a superior apart from obedience to him, and Jesus Christ is very much our Superior.

Before I became a Christian I spent some time on the island of Pavuvu with the First Marine Division during World War II. Pavuvu was our rest camp between invasions. And what a rest camp it was! The island was infested with blow flies, red ants, and mosquitoes. Our tents leaked and in the mornings we would often find land crabs in our boots. The heat was oppressive and the daily rain was a nuisance. We had nothing but "C" rations to eat.

To make life a bit more bearable, the Marine Corps provided

one can of beer a month, much to the delight of us beer drinkers. Though we welcomed this monthly treat, it hardly filled the bill for those of us who were used to beer as a steady diet. So I hit upon a little scheme. When the beer ration was given, I worked it out with the non-drinkers to sell me theirs. This was strictly against the regulations of course, but in our outfit it was pretty well recognized that a good conduct medal meant four years of undetected rule breaking.

I would take my 12-15 cans of warm beer back to my tent, sit in the middle of the floor, poke them open with a rusty Japanese bayonet, and start consuming the contents. After 8-10 cans I would usually get a bit unsteady and would begin shaking the can a bit before opening it. One day I dropped a can a couple of times, finally got it upright, and hit it with the bayonet. It spurted a stream of warm beer—all over my commanding officer who at that moment had stepped into my tent. There he stood, drenched from head to foot with my warm beer. Somehow for the next few weeks he and I didn't experience the warmth of fellowship that we had known.

There *is* no fellowship with a superior apart from obedience. Jesus said, "He that hath My commandments, and keepeth them, he it is that loveth Me: and he that loveth Me shall be loved of My Father, and I will love him, and will manifest Myself to him" (John 14:21).

The danger of disobedience was clearly spelled out by our Lord. "And why call ye Me, 'Lord, Lord,' and do not the things which I say? Whosoever cometh to Me, and heareth My sayings, and doeth them, I will show you to whom he is like: he is like a man which built an house, and digged deep, and laid the foundation on a rock: and when the flood arose, the stream beat vehemently upon that house, and could not shake it: for it was founded upon a rock. But he that heareth, and doeth not is like a man that without a foundation built an house upon the earth; against which the stream did beat vehemently, and immediately it fell; and the ruin of that house was great" (Luke 6:46-49). A life of obedience by the leader is the greatest motivation to the people who follow him. They see his life and are challenged to greater heights of commitment and obedience.

The three elements of fellowship are the Word, prayer, and obedience. They are absolute imperatives for the leader. He needs to experience the power of God in his life and ministry on a day by day basis. Fellowship with the Lord is the switch that completes the connection and makes that power available. Without it the leader is nothing more than an organizer of human effort and activity. With it he is a tool in the hands of Almighty God to be used to accomplish His purposes on this earth.

3

The Inner Life
of the Leader

The Babylonians were a brutal people. Their code of morality and justice was strange and foreign to the captive Hebrews. Killing a human being to them was no different than swatting a fly. Yet here were the Hebrews, terror-stricken slaves in that cruel land, confronted by rules, regulations, and demands that were contrary to everything they had been taught from youth. They were up against what appeared to be insurmountable odds; yet one of their number would rise to a position of power and authority—in an empire filled with violence, superstition, and the worship of false gods. During the years of his captivity this man would be called upon by pagan kings to serve in the highest appointive office in the land. The most remarkable thing of all is that he was a man of unbending principle who worshiped the living and true God. We can learn much by looking at the inner life of this remarkable leader.

Daniel was only a youth when he was chosen by King Nebuchadnezzar for a special assignment. He was one of a small group "whom they might teach the learning and the tongue of the Chaldeans" (Dan 1:4). He and his three companions were part of an elite band of young men with very special qualifications: "Children in whom was no blemish, but well favored, and skilful in all wisdom, and cunning in knowledge, and understanding science, and such as had ability in them to stand in the king's palace" (Dan. 1:4). Stated in contemporary language, they were physically fit, socially desirable, practically intelligent (they had horse sense), intellectually sharp, educationally equipped, and diplomatically capable.

Any dean of admissions of any college or university would look at this list of qualifications and welcome such youths to the student body. Corporations would drool at the prospect of getting young men like these in their employ. But here's an interesting thing: God raised up only one of them to the place of greatest spiritual leadership. Why? Because of certain basic qualities in the inner life of this man. Let us examine three of the most important.

Purity of Life

A primary characteristic exhibited by Daniel was purity of life. "Daniel purposed in his heart that he would not defile himself" (Dan. 1:8). It is interesting to note that one of the first things God did at the dawn of creation was to divide the light from the darkness. That act symbolizes a great spiritual truth: you're either on one side or the other—there's no room for fence-straddling.

In hell there is no light, and in heaven there is no darkness. We, who have given our lives to Christ, having experienced His love and forgiveness, will one day live with Him in heaven; we will enter His mansions and bask in His presence. In preparation for that great day, we ought to get used to walking in the light while on this earth.

The Apostle Paul continues this theme: "Be ye not unequally yoked together with unbelievers; for what fellowship hath righteousness with unrighteousness? and what communion hath light with darkness? And what concord hath Christ with Belial? or what part hath he that believeth with an infidel? And what agreement hath the temple of God with idols? for ye are the temple of the living God" (2 Cor. 6:14-16).

Paul used the five questions just quoted to draw a line of demarcation between God and the opposition. On one side he gathers righteousness, light, Christ, faith, and the house of God. On the other he lists lawlessness, darkness, Satan, unbelief, and false worship. He states that you cannot mix these two lists. You must choose to live on one side or the other. This is an obvious truth; yet many of us attempt to compromise with sin. The leader must set an example in his own behavior that matches the standard of Scripture: "A bishop then must be blameless" (1 Tim. 3:2).

The Lord takes note of the inner life of the leader and it has always been so. When God had rejected King Saul and was choosing his successor, He said to Samuel, "Look not on his countenance, or on the height of his stature; because I have refused him: for the Lord seeth not as man seeth; for man looketh on the outward appearance, but the Lord looketh on the heart" (1 Sam. 16:7). You and I tend to evaluate people by superficial standards: only what we see. God looks inside.

Some months ago a violent windstorm hit our city. It blew out plate glass windows in the downtown stores and banks. Herb Lockyer, the man who teaches our Sunday School class, and his wife Ardis were driving home when she saw something that caused her heart to sink. One of the most beautiful trees in town had been uprooted by the wind. She called it to Herb's attention and then exclaimed, "Look Herb! That tree is rotten on the inside."

It was true. This tree that had been admired for its grandeur and beauty was completely eaten out on the inside. And because it was rotten within, there came a day when it faced a wind it could not withstand. It toppled, and people who had appreciated its huge branches and beautiful leaves learned the truth. In spite of the fact that outwardly it was a thing of beauty, inwardly it was rotten.

So it is with our lives. If the Christian leader tries to put on an outward show with no inward fortification of purity and holiness before God, one day a test will reveal his true nature and character. Thus, the leader *must* live a pure life.

Paul shares with Timothy another reason for moral purity. "Let every one that nameth the name of Christ depart from iniquity. But in a great house there are not only vessels of gold and of silver, but also of wood and of earth; and some to honor, and some to dishonor. If a man therefore purge himself from these, he shall be a vessel unto honor, sanctified, and meet for the master's use, and prepared unto every good work" (2 Tim. 2:19-21).

This passage points out a truth that is obvious in our homes. Various receptacles have various uses. In my home we have one container for garbage and another that is used as a salad bowl. And my wife doesn't mix them up and change them around. The simple spiritual truth is that a man can choose which kind of vessel he will be in the household of God. It is up to him to be a vessel unto honor or dishonor. The criteria by which God decides whom He will use for which of His eternal purposes on earth are spelled out at the end (v. 21): those who purge themselves of dishonorable characteristics will be vessels unto honor.

Some years ago my wife's uncle Art gave her a lovely set of old crystal glasses. These occupy a place of honor in our household and are used only on very special occasions. Suppose you were visiting me and became thirsty. I would take you to the kitchen and invite you to help yourself to a cool refreshing drink from the faucet. As you opened the cupboard to get a glass you would see that each of these fine crystal glasses was smeared and dirty. Right in front of you on the counter you'd see a plain old peanut butter jar that was as clean as a whistle. Which one would you use?

The answer is obvious. Well, you are no smarter than God. He is looking for a life that is clean and pure. Then that life will be "a vessel unto honor, sanctified, and meet for the master's use, perfected unto every good work."

Notice the word *sanctified*. Much disagreement exists among God's people regarding that word, but all will agree that one of its basic meanings is "to be set apart." Let me illustrate. I have a friend who is a ranking officer in the Marine Corps. Wherever he is stationed he is given a jeep for his personal use. This jeep is always available to him and he knows where it is when he needs it. Woe be to any young second lieutenant who would take that jeep for his own purposes. That jeep is *sanctified*. It belongs to the major and is for his use alone.

The leader whose life is set apart for the Lord has a powerful impact on the world around him. God has promised to show Himself to others *through* that leader. " 'And I will sanctify My great name, which was profaned among the heathen, which ye have profaned in the midst of them; and the heathen shall know that I am the Lord,' saith the Lord God, 'when I shall be sanctified in you before their eyes' " (Ezek. 36:23).

Often the leader is asked by his people for specifics in determining what is right and what is wrong. They want to lead pure lives but are honestly unsure of some issues. The Bible not only deals in specifics, but in eternal principles. Four of these have been used by the Lord in my own life.

Shortly after I came to know Christ, I realized that certain habits and practices in my life needed to go. I knew they were wrong and did not honor the Lord. Some other things were not so clear. Were they wrong, or weren't they? The Bible was specific about swearing, stealing, and lying, but what about those doubtful things concerning which the Bible gives no clear word?

Shortly after I began to wonder about this, the Lord gave me three verses of Scripture that have been of tremendous help through the years. They contain "how to know right from wrong" principles. I call them the 6—8—10 principles, because they are found in 1 Corinthians 6, 8, and 10.

1. *Is it helpful?* "All things are lawful unto me, but all things are not expedient; all things are lawful for me, but I will not be brought under the power of any" (1 Cor. 6:12). On the basis of that verse, I can ask myself: Is it helpful? Is whatever I'm about to do helpful to me *physically,* or will it harm me? Does it help me *mentally,* or does it tend to get my mind on things that draw me into sin? This helped me get guidance with regard to motion pictures, TV programs, and certain books and magazines. And, does it help me *spiritually?* Does it help me grow, or does it hurt my spiritual development?

2. *Does it get me in its power?* Does it enslave me? I concluded from that verse (1 Cor. 6:12) that anything that gets me in its grip—that becomes a habit I cannot break—I should leave alone. I have friends today who are slaves to cigarettes, liquor, and drugs. Paul said, "I will not be brought under the power of any[thing]."

3. *Will it cause others to stumble?* "But when ye sin so against the brethren, and wound their weak conscience, ye sin against Christ. Wherefore, if meat make my brother to offend, I will eat no flesh while the world standeth, lest I make my brother to offend" (1 Cor. 8:12-13). Will my doing this cause others to stumble? Maybe I can handle it, but will it affect others who see me doing it? Will it cause them problems? Will my actions lead them into trouble? No man is an island. What I do is seen and sometimes copied by others. And I am the only example of a Christian that somebody has. So I must think of others when I decide on my activities.

4. *Is it glorifying to God?* "Whether therefore ye eat, or drink, or whatsoever ye do, do all to the glory of God" (1 Cor. 10:31). Does this contemplated action glorify God? Note the first question in the Westminster Shorter Catechism. "What is the chief end of man?" The answer: "Man's chief end is to glorify God and to enjoy Him forever." You and I are to live our lives to the praise of His glory. So I must ask myself: Can I do this to the glory of God?

These three passages of Scripture have stood the test of time.

They contain lasting principles from the all-knowing and ever-loving God.

The question God asks, then, is what's on the inside. Outward performance will reflect the inner life. The leader must maintain a godly walk before his people and make frequent application of 1 John 1:9: "If we confess our sins He is faithful and just to forgive us our sins and to cleanse us from all unrighteousness."

Humility
Another vital characteristic in considering the inner life of the leader is humility. Facing a situation in which most of us would have been content just to stay alive, Daniel rose to a place of power and influence. Under his leadership the kingdom prospered, and he was able to provide guidance and instruction for the king. Through it all, however, he remained a humble servant of God. Often, when he could have exalted himself, he was content to give all the credit to the Lord. "Daniel answered in the presence of the king, and said, 'The secret which the king hath demanded cannot the wise men, the astrologers, the magicians, the soothsayers, show unto the king; but there is a God in heaven that revealeth secrets, and maketh known to the king Nebuchadnezzar what shall be in the latter days. Thy dream, and the visions of thy head upon thy bed, are these; as for thee, O king, thy thoughts came into thy mind upon thy bed, what should come to pass hereafter: and He that revealeth secrets maketh known to thee what shall come to pass. But as for me, this secret is not revealed to me for any wisdom that I have more than any living, but for their sakes that shall make known the interpretation to the king, and that thou mightest know the thoughts of thy heart'" (Dan. 2:27-30).

A humble spirit is the hallmark of the man God uses. God requires it in His servant. "I am the Lord: that is My name: and My glory will I not give to another, neither my praise to graven images" (Isa. 42:8). When His men deviate from the path in this regard and get proud, God has a way of bringing them back to the straight and narrow.

One summer I had the privilege of visiting the foreign mission field. One of the missionaries there told me a fascinating tale.

It seems that when he left for the field, he considered himself God's gift to the world and to the country where he went. His basic attitude was, "Wait till I get there. I'll show 'em! Once I get there I'll be able to straighten everyone out and get the program really producing." So he arrived and began his work.

Needless to say his attitude toward his co-workers did not especially endear him to their hearts. They saw his proud spirit and were turned off. Worst of all, God took note of it and did not prosper his efforts. Nothing went right. All his visionary plans turned to dust. Scripture says, "Likewise, ye younger, submit yourselves unto the elder. Yea, all of you be subject one to another, and be clothed with humility: for God resisteth the proud, and giveth grace to the humble. Humble yourselves therefore under the mighty hand of God, that He may exalt you in due time" (1 Peter 5:5-6). God *resists,* not blesses, the proud, and the Lord is a formidable Person to have resisting you! Needless to say, the missionary lost.

The story has a happy ending, however. The man saw the error of his ways, repented of his sin, and began to walk humbly with his God. And his life became a blessing. "He hath showed thee, O man, what is good; and what doth the Lord require of thee, but to do justly, and to love mercy, and to walk humbly with thy God" (Micah 6:8).

Many passages of Scripture deal with this subject. Here are some crucial ones:

Proverbs 6:16-17: "These . . . things doth the Lord hate: yea, [they] are an abomination unto Him: A proud look, a lying tongue, and hands that shed innocent blood." Note what heads the list!

Proverbs 8:13: "The fear of the Lord is to hate evil: pride and arrogancy, and the evil way, and the froward mouth, do I hate." Mark well what is at the top.

Why does God oppose pride so vehemently? Is it just some meaningless guideline that the Lord issued? No, of course not. As with everything else in the Scriptures, when the Lord tries to get us to conform to His standards, it is for our own well-being. The way to a full and happy life is to get our eyes off ourselves and live for others. The leader will prosper only as he walks in that spirit. Pride is one of the prime tools of the devil to get our eyes on ourselves and off others.

When you are looking at yourself, you become insensitive to the needs of other people. You find yourself going through life hurting others, offending them, using them, and abusing them, perhaps even without knowing it. I have observed this in the life of men in positions of leadership, and it has been a tragic thing to watch their spiritual decline.

Philippians 2:3-4: "Let nothing be done through strife or vainglory; but in lowliness of mind let each esteem other better than themselves. Look not every man on his own things, but every man also on the things of others."

A clear example of the corrosive effect of pride may be seen in the life of Uzziah, one of the kings of Judah. "Sixteen years old was Uzziah when he began to reign, and he reigned 52 years in Jerusalem. His mother's name also was Jecoliah of Jerusalem" (2 Chron. 26:3). At first his basic heart attitude was pure. "And he sought God in the days of Zechariah, who had understanding in the visions of God: and as long as he sought the Lord, God made him to prosper" (v. 5). He became famous and successful. "And the Ammonites gave gifts to Uzziah: and his name spread abroad even to the entering in of Egypt; for he strengthened himself exceedingly" (v. 8). He developed mighty armies and God blessed him.

Then came the beginning of his downfall. "But when he was strong, his heart was lifted up to his destruction: for he transgressed against the Lord his God, and went into the temple of the Lord to burn incense upon the altar of incense" (v. 16). The problem? He couldn't manage success. He was overcome by pride. And God struck him down with leprosy.

A leader must be able to define and communicate his objectives and then determine the best path to follow to reach those goals. Pride is his greatest enemy at that juncture. When a man is full of pride he cannot see the best way of achieving his purposes, for he only sees the way that brings *him* the most honor and acclaim. Somehow pride blinds a person to finding the best path. His mind refuses to be that discerning. He sees only what his pride wants him to see. And it has deadly consequences.

King Nebuchadnezzar fell because of it. "But when his heart was lifted up, and his mind hardened in pride, he was deposed from his kingly throne, and they took his glory from him" (Dan. 5:20).

On the other hand, Isaiah portrays the kind of man God uses. "Thus saith the Lord, 'The heaven is My throne, and the earth is My footstool: where is the house that ye build unto Me? and where is the place of My rest? For all those things hath Mine hand made, and all those things have been,' saith the Lord: 'but to this man will I look, even to him that is poor and of a contrite spirit, and trembleth at My word' " (Isa. 66:1-2). I have heard Billy Graham say on numerous occasions, that he gives all the glory to God for whatever is accomplished through his ministry. He states emphatically that if he touches that glory, he is finished.

A proud spirit, therefore, is deadly to the leader. It will kill his effectiveness for God for it breeds two dreadful diseases of the soul. The first is *ignorance*. Pride makes a man self-sufficient and unteachable. It blinds him to his own needs. It causes him to ignore the good advice and counsel of others.

Throughout the Scriptures God directs our attention to the tremendous value of counsel. "Without counsel purposes are disappointed: but in the multitude of counsellors they are established" (Prov. 15:22).

Spiritual counsel, however, must be that which has the Lord's interest at heart. That which is best for the kingdom of God. Many seek advice only from those who agree with them; others are disappointed became they can't find unbiased counsel. Counsel, even when given by someone who truly loves you and is interested in that which is best for you can be dead wrong.

I recall discussing this with G. Christian Weiss, a respected missionary statesman and Director of Missions for Back to the Bible Broadcast. He told me that he would not have gone to the mission field had he listened to the advice of his friends and relatives. They felt he was throwing his life away. They loved him and had *his* best interest in mind.

The leader must have these things before him when he is giving and receiving counsel. He must be teachable but not gullible. He must weigh the counsel he receives in the light of the Bible and the welfare of God's kingdom. His heart must remain open and teachable to others. "Where no counsel is, the people fall: but in the multitude of counsellors there is safety" (Prov. 11:14).

The second disease caused by pride is *insecurity*. The leader with his eyes on himself has excessive concern about how he appears in the eyes of others. He is constantly measuring himself by the yardstick of other people's performances. The Word of God states that this is a foolish and unwise practice. "For we dare not make ourselves of the number, or compare ourselves with some that commend themselves: but they measuring themselves by themselves, and comparing themselves among themselves, are not wise" (2 Cor. 10:12).

Instead of relaxing in the blessed knowledge that "God set the members every one of them in the body as it hath pleased Him," the insecure leader constantly worries about what others think of him. This makes him less effective in his job because his eyes are no longer on the objectives. His co-workers become a threat to him rather than a help.

Two extremes can result. He will either try to impress others with ambitious plans and big programs designed to "show them what he can do," or he will retreat into inaction. If he launches a big program, it is likely to be prompted by the energy of the flesh and will ultimately fail. I recall watching a man do this with tragic results. It was like watching a giant factory in full production. The dust was flying, the machines were running, the people were busy, but nothing was coming off the assembly line. The leader's insecurity led him to promote a flurry of activity, but it lacked the blessing of God.

The other extreme, of course, is the fear of failure that brings everything to a standstill. Rather than admit his weaknesses and step out in faith, he does nothing. The Apostle Paul realized his own weakness, but found it to be an asset in his work for Christ when he had the proper attitude: "For this thing I besought the Lord thrice, that it might depart from me. And He said unto me, 'My grace is sufficient for thee: for My strength is made perfect in weakness.' Most gladly therefore will I rather glory in my infirmities, that the power of Christ may rest upon me" (2 Cor. 12:8-9). A humble spirit in the life of the leader is a powerful force in the hands of almighty God.

How does a leader maintain a humble spirit before the Lord? Many things are involved, of course, but one stands out. To walk humbly before God one needs to live a life of genuine *praise*. In heaven the beings who surround the throne of God cry, "Holy, Holy, Holy, Lord God Almighty" (Rev. 4:8). If the leader lives in that spirit of praise he will be reminded of his own sinfulness and weaknesses. But the reminder will not be from an unhealthy introspection. It will come from a heart that is filled with praises to God for His holiness and power. This in turn can be used of God to thrust him out in faith, confident in the promise, "I can do all things through Christ which strengtheneth me" (Phil. 4:13).

Faith
The third vital characteristic in the inner life of the leader is

faith. The Bible says, "But without faith it is impossible to please Him; for he that cometh to God must believe that He is, and that He is a rewarder of them that diligently seek Him" (Heb. 11:6). So often we hear that God looks for a child-like faith in His followers. But what is that? What is involved? We will discuss four aspects.

First, faith means that we *believe God will provide.* "But my God shall supply all your need according to His riches in glory by Christ Jesus" (Phil. 4:19). My first assignment as a Christian worker was in Pittsburgh. I arrived with the shirt on my back and that was about all. Finances were tight and my needs were many.

Our home was to be used extensively in the ministry, but the living room was bare except for a davenport in front of the window. So my wife, a young minister named Ken Smith, and I decided to pray for the specific needs of our living room. We prayed for two end tables, a coffee table, and a chair for the corner.

The next day the phone rang. A man asked for Ken and said, "Rev. Smith, I don't know if you remember me or not, but you witnessed to me downtown the other day. Well, I'm being transferred to Buffalo, N.Y., where I've got a job sandblasting. I've arranged to dispose of most of my furniture, but there are some pieces I just can't get rid of. I hope you won't be offended, but I got to thinking maybe you could use them. Could you find any use for two end tables, a coffee table, and a corner chair?"

Ken dropped the phone. He picked it up and answered the man that we'd be right over. We rented a trailer and by that afternoon the room was furnished.

We lived on the north side of town and it was difficult to get to the university on the east side. I spent eight hours a day on campus witnessing to students and really needed a car. Ray Joseph, a young seminary student, and I were meeting regularly at five A.M. on Wednesdays to pray about our lives and ministries. One morning we prayed specifically that God would provide a car to get me to campus.

The following Wednesday night the phone rang. It was a lady from First Presbyterian Church, who taught a class of adults. She said that one of the men in the class, Bill Newton, was getting a new car. The offer on the trade-in was so small that he wanted to give it to someone in need. Their class had heard I was working at the university and wondered if I could use a car. I told her that as a matter of fact I had been praying for a car.

She said, "Your prayers are answered!"

Bill and Edie Newton not only gave us the car, but the whole class pitched in $125 to get the motor fixed, buy insurance for a year, secure the license plates, and to top it all off gave us $50 for gasoline.

I had moved to Pittsburgh from the West Coast and soon discovered that my clothing was a bit out of style at this prestigious Eastern school. The students wore dark grey single-breasted suits, black and grey neckties, and black shoes and socks. Each Monday night we ate dinner in a different fraternity house and presented the Gospel. In the midst of this sea of black I stood out like a roman candle. I had a light green double-breasted suit, a colorful flowered necktie, and a pair of yellow crepe-soled shoes. So I began to pray about my wardrobe. Within a week God provided a dark suit that fit perfectly. The following week Ken Smith and I were helping an elderly lady in his church with some chores around her house. As we finished the job and were walking out, she stuffed a paper sack under my arm. On the way home I opened the sack and discovered a pair of black shoes that fit perfectly.

Another need I had was a watch. Mine had been broken that summer by some kids in a Vacation Bible School I had led in my hometown of Neola, Iowa. Because I had no watch I was occasionally late for appointments and knew that this dishonored the Lord. So I prayed.

One night I spoke to the Saturday Night Bible Class that had been started through the ministry of Dr. Donald G. Barnhouse. The following Wednesday night a member of that class came to our house with a thank-you gift. It was a box about the size of Halley's Bible Handbook and I was delighted. But when I opened it I discovered it was not a handbook but a wristwatch, an Omega Automatic that I still have. To me as a young Christian leader in a strange city, God showed over and over again that He was ready, willing, and able to provide for my needs.

Faith also means that we *believe that what we do for God will prosper.* "And he shall be like a tree planted by the rivers of water, that bringeth forth his fruit in his season; his leaf also shall not wither; and whatsoever he doeth shall prosper" (Ps. 1:3).

Our property has a creek running through it—a creek surrounded by weeds, trees, and wild flowers. My wife's garden, her pride and joy, is back there as well. She cares for it constantly. When a plant looks unhealthy, she nurtures it back to health with water and plant food or fertilizer. However, she does not crawl down into the creek to care for the trees and bushes that are growing wild. Her eye is constantly on the things *she* has planted. The Bible teaches that we are not wild plants growing here and there. We are "trees planted" by our heavenly Father. We are under His constant care and protection, surrounded by the rivers of His love, mercy, and grace.

The psalmist emphasizes this truth again: "He will not suffer thy foot to be moved: He that keepeth thee will not slumber. Behold, He that keepeth Israel shall neither slumber nor sleep. The Lord is thy keeper: the Lord is thy shade upon thy right hand" (Ps. 121:3-5).

Recently I read of an incident in the life of a famous sea captain during the days of the great sailing vessels. He was crossing the Atlantic from Liverpool to New York when the ship ran into a fierce storm. The waves were gigantic, the wind blew with hurricane force, and the ship was violently tossed about.

The passengers were terror-stricken, pulling on their life vests and preparing for the worst. The captain's eight-year-old daughter was aboard that trip. She was awakened by the noise and cried out in alarm asking what was wrong. They told her of the storm, and the perilous condition of the ship.

She asked, "Is my father on deck?"

They assured her that he was.

She smiled, laid her head back on her pillow, and was asleep in minutes.

This is the kind of child-like faith that pleases God. He assures us that He keeps our souls, that He never slumbers nor sleeps.

Faith further means that we *believe God to be absolutely trustworthy*. This was illustrated once by my youngest son. He had outgrown his little bike and wanted a bigger one. We went down to the bike shop and looked them all over. He didn't nag and whine when we discussed whether we could afford one or not. His attitude was, "Whatever you think is best, Dad."

"Righteous art Thou, O Lord, and upright are Thy judgments. Thy testimonies that Thou hast commanded are righteous and very faithful" (Ps. 119:137-138). God has never done a single wrong thing. What He calls upon us to believe and do is absolutely right. His Word is utterly trustworthy. What He decides, where He leads, and what He says is right. His promises are sure. His will is good, acceptable, and perfect.

In addition to relying on the promises, protection, and trustworthiness of God, we can discern another beam shining from the character of God and related to faith: *God's power*. This summer I was meditating on the story of the father and child as recorded in Mark 9. Jesus and three of the disciples had come from the Mount of Transfiguration to find a discouraging scene. The father had brought the child to other of Jesus' disciples for help, but they were unable to do any good. Jesus asked the father how long the condition had existed.

The father answered, "Of a child" (v. 21). He continued, "And ofttimes it [the demon] hath cast him into the fire, and into the waters, to destroy him: but if Thou canst do *anything,* have compassion on us, and help us" (v. 22). Notice the word *anything*. The father would have been satisfied with any sort of help.

But Jesus answered, "If thou canst believe, all things are possible to him that believeth" (v. 23).

His answer is fascinating. The father had said, "If Thou canst do." Jesus answered, "If thou canst believe." The father says "anything"; Jesus answered "all things." The problem is never what or how much Jesus can do. The problem rests in what we can believe. As Jesus told two blind men on another occasion, "According to your faith be it unto you" (Matt. 9:29).

The inner life of the leader will either make him or break him. If he neglects the cultivation of purity, humility, and faith, he is in for big trouble. On the other hand, if anyone sets himself to be God's kind of man, "the eyes of the Lord run to and fro throughout the whole earth, to show Himself strong in the behalf of them whose heart is perfect toward Him" (2 Chron. 16:9). By God's grace you can be such a man.

4

The Leader's Attitude Toward Others

As the previous chapter explains, the outward performance and success of a Christian leader depends for the most part on his inner life. No man who is self-serving, proud, lazy, or hypocritical *should* have followers. We will now look at the inner life of the leader in another area: his basic attitudes toward others.

The Apostle Paul said, "Now the end of the commandment is [love] out of a pure heart, and of a good conscience, and of faith unfeigned" (1 Tim. 1:5). The ultimate objective of all of his instruction was to produce love toward others, a good conscience in themselves, and true faith in God. This is the basis of a life of joy. J-O-Y, *J*esus first, *O*thers second, and *Y*ourself last.

Let's look at the crucial inner characteristics that will most enhance the leader's relationships with those who follow.

A Servant Heart

Jesus gave us the basic summary of His life: "For even the Son of man came not to be ministered unto, but to minister, and to give His life a ransom for many" (Mark 10:45). He was among us as One who served (see Luke 22:27).

Today it is not possible for us to serve the Lord by taking a sacrificial animal to the side of a hill, kindling a fire, and presenting it to Him. To serve God we must serve others, as Jesus did. The leader must offer his own life on the altar of God to be consumed in the flame of God's love, in service to others. "Hereby perceive we the love of God, because He laid down His life for us: and we ought to lay down our lives for the brethren" (1 John 3:16).

This, of course, is contrary to the practice of most secular leadership. Go into any business office where the organizational chart of the firm is displayed and you will see that the leader has his name at the top with lines running from top to bottom. And in most cases he and the higher echelons of management demand service from others.

Jesus came and reversed the direction of service without giving up His leadership. He told His apostles: "Ye know that the princes of the Gentiles exercise dominion over them, and they that are great exercise authority upon them. But it shall not be so among you: but whosoever will be great among you, let him be your minister; and whosoever will be chief among you, let him be your servant; Even as the Son of man came not to be ministered unto, but to minister, and to give His life a ransom for many" (Matt. 20:25-28).

Much of the teaching of Christ was revolutionary and strange to the hearers of His day. His teaching regarding leadership continues to have an unfamiliar ring in an age that calls for us to climb to the top. The Bible teaches that to lead is to serve. In our more spiritual moments we recognize the truth of this concept and respond with a warm, positive attitude. The problem, however, arises in the day-to-day doing of it. It is so much easier to let the other person bring the iced tea on a hot muggy day. How long has it been since we've shined somebody's shoes for him—to say nothing of washing his feet!

One evening my wife and I served a fish dinner to about 20 men. Some of the guys had been to the lake and returned with about 40 beautiful rainbow trout. We topped the meal off with gallons of homemade ice cream. After we had eaten our fill, one of the fellows suggested they help with the clean up. Great idea!

As the men organized themselves into furniture straighteners, floor cleaners, garbage haulers, and dishwashers, I saw a sight that was hard to believe. One of the fellows who had eaten the most and enjoyed it to the fullest got up from his chair, walked over to the window, and hid behind the drapes. That's right! *He hid behind the drapes!*

After the work was organized and well underway, he stepped out, moved to a chair, sat down, and began to read a magazine. Remember the statement of Jesus, "I am among you as He that serveth"? (Luke 22:27) This fellow had it turned around.

There is always room for one more servant. The small area in the spotlight can get a bit crowded, but there is always room in the shadows for the person who is eager to serve.

Stephen was a man full of faith and power, and the enemies of Christ were not able to resist the wisdom and the spirit by which he spoke. He had a remarkable grasp of the Word of God and the boldness to preach it with conviction. One day the apostles came to him and asked if he would serve tables for some Grecian widows who were being neglected in the daily distribution of food.

Stephen could have said, "Me? Serve tables? Apparently you are unaware of my wisdom, power, faith, and preaching ability. Get someone else to stand in the shadows and serve. I'm sure you can see that I am better suited to the spotlight in center stage."

But no, thank God, that was not his reaction. He eagerly took his place among the six other servants and waited on tables. I'm sure that is one of the prime reasons he has held a place in God's spotlight down through the centuries. Only one person could be the first martyr in the cause of Christ and Stephen is it. No one can ever replace him.

The Bible teaches that the way up is down. "But he that is greatest among you shall be your servant. And whosoever shall exalt himself shall be abased; and he that shall humble himself shall be exalted" (Matt. 23:11-12).

A Sensitive Spirit

A second necessary attitude of the leader toward others might be described as a sensitive spirit. Jesus again is our best example of this. Observe His reaction to people's needs. "In those days the multitude being very great, and having nothing to eat, Jesus called His disciples unto Him, and saith unto them, 'I have compassion on the multitude, because they have now been with Me three days, and have nothing to eat: And if I send them away fasting to their own houses, they will faint by the way:' for divers of them had come from far" (Mark 8:1-3).

Jesus knew how long a person could go without food. He had fasted 40 days and nights in the wilderness. But he didn't look around at the multitude and insist that they gather for another meeting. He could have told them, "Don't talk to Me about hunger. I know what hunger is. I went for 40 days without food, and these people have only been out here for three days. Tell them to stop complaining. We have just begun."

This is a common failing among men in leadership positions. They evaluate their own capacities and expect everybody else to keep up with them. But that's not the way it is. Many sincere Christians who have warm hearts toward the Lord are limited in their abilities. They need a slightly slower pace and a shorter distance. Because the leader can work harder longer, has a greater capacity for prayer, and more intense hunger for the Word, he can usually out-distance those around him. That's what makes him the leader.

So a leader must be sensitive to the needs of the people and compassionate in his dealing with them. One thing he must do above all else: get to know them as individuals.

One day last year my son came home from school. I told him about my day and how things had gone. Then he began to tell me about his. He mentioned how much he liked a certain teacher, so I asked him why.

It was simple. "Dad, he knows my name." Amazing! It had nothing to do with the man's ability or background. He didn't say whether the man was loud or quiet, gentle or tough. The teacher knew Randy's name. That's all.

But the Lord spoke to me through that situation. People hunger to be recognized. Not only that, the leader if he's worth his salt must get to know them. It is the only way he can do them any good or lead meaningfully.

The Scriptures clearly teach that we must deal with people according to their individual characteristics. "Now we exhort you, brethren, warn them that are unruly, comfort the feebleminded, support the weak, be patient toward all men" (1 Thes. 5:14).

Three types of people are mentioned in this passage. The first are those who need to be held in line—the *unruly.*

A shepherd would certainly understand this aspect of leadership, spending his days in keeping the foolish sheep from hurting themselves or going astray. "He chose David also His servant, and took him from the sheepfolds; from following the ewes great with young He brought him to feed Jacob His people, and Israel His inheritance. So he fed them according to the integrity of his heart; and guided them by the skillfulness of his hands" (Ps. 78: 70-72).

Perhaps the "unruly" includes those who when faced with a problem or difficulty want to throw in the towel and quit. They could go on, but they find it easier not to. Possibly they were offended by someone and want to pick up their marbles and go home. This of course is the reaction of a person who is immature. He has to be handled with kid gloves. The reason? He's a kid. But, he does need to be helped and the leader must stick with him. It requires an overload of patience and earnest prayer, but it can be done.

The second group mentioned are the *feebleminded,* or, better, the fainthearted, the timid. These are the people who tend to be afraid of their own shadows. They need to be led to the place where they are able to take a step of faith, and eventually launch out into the deep and experience the trustworthiness of God.

The greatest help to these people is to hear testimonies of others who have been over the road and who have found the Lord faithful. God can use these testimonies to build courage into the lives of the timid.

A Bible study for women meets in our city, led by Mrs. Morena Downing. Morena has walked with the Lord for many years and her radiant testimony and deep faith in God have been an inspiration to many—including me. Her class has grown quite large and scores of women testify that it is through Morena's leadership that they have sort of "come out of their shell."

Many now feel confident in witnessing. Others are bold in their stand for righteousness and truth, even when such a stand is not popular. As a result, numerous people have met the Saviour through the lives of these women. Morena has truly strengthened the "fainthearted."

Harvey Oslund is a Christian leader in our nation's capital whose life has been mightily blessed of God. Today many men and women who have been reached and trained by this man are serving the Lord around the world. One of his strengths is the ability to inspire people to give sacrificially to God.

Again, it is not so much what Harvey says but what he is. His life, his money, all that he has and is has been given to God. He is one of the most generous men I have ever met. I have talked to people who have learned the joy of giving because of his example. Before they met Harv they were afraid to give; they sat on their billfolds while hesitantly putting a small coin in the collection plate. Seeing Harv's life changed all that for them. Today their lives are marked by sacrifice and generosity. When special needs come along they dig deep, take bold steps of faith, and experience the joys of giving.

Remember, "It is more blessed to give than to receive" (Acts 20:35). Timid, hesitant, reluctant non-givers have become bold, joyful givers. How? Once "fainthearted," they were challenged by the life of a man who was setting the pace. His life and testimony inspired them, strengthened them, and enabled them to change.

The last group mentioned are people who are *weak*. I believe this refers to believers who are plagued by besetting sins. The instruction is: "Help the weak." Here again are people who need special attention, often personal, individual help. Quite frequently they are most helped by the opportunity to talk over their weaknesses with someone they trust, and who they know will keep the conversation in confidence. It is a frightening thing to hear a story you shared with your leader repeated to the whole group, even though the names have been changed to protect the guilty!

The fact that a Christian has a lingering battle with a sin that plagues him is certainly no indication that he lacks potential usefulness to the Lord. Dawson Trotman, founder of The Navigators, often told of his battle with profanity as a young Christian. He would determine to stop, only to fail again and again. Eventually, through the patient love and fervent prayers of a godly Sunday School teacher, he was able to overcome the habit by the help of the Lord.

Rod Sargent is a man mightily used of God throughout the world today. As a young Christian, however, he experienced many difficulties because of his alcoholism. Before his conversion he spent many a night in Los Angeles bars, to wake up next morning with splitting headaches followed by terrifying blackouts. He came to Christ through a Christian fellowship in Pasadena, and continued to meet with the group for Bible study and prayer. But he would occasionally succumb to the old temptation and go to a bar for a few drinks.

This double life brought on the fear that the group would find out and no longer welcome him. The leader of the group, however, knew what was going on, but continued to meet with Rod for prayer and fellowship in the Word. He practiced the scriptural admonition, "Help the weak." Today Rod is himself a respected Christian leader. The man who had helped him had a sensitive spirit, knew Rod's need, and met it.

Get to know the people you would lead. Know those who need to have a fire built under them to get them moving and those who need to be held back. Some have great talents and need to put them to work. Others are prone to tackle things that are a bit beyond their abilities and capacities. If allowed to plunge ahead they will likely find themselves over their heads in responsibilities and demands that are beyond them.

These two things, then, a servant heart and a sensitive spirit, are crucial for a good leader. If you are to lead, these characteristics must be an integral part of your life. "Give therefore Thy servant an understanding heart to judge Thy people, that I may discern between good and bad: for who is able to judge this Thy so great a people?" (1 Kings 3:9-10)

5

Why Some Leaders Excel

The good is the enemy of the best. Too often when people are asked about a class or a series of meetings or a calling program, they reply, "Oh, it was OK." Some may say, "It was terrible!" This is almost a consolation, for all too often responses seem to fall into that bland ground of mediocrity. Satisfaction with the status quo shows that a program is really in trouble. This is especially true when the leader knows there is apathy and is content to have it so.

On the other hand, some programs stand out visibly. They are fresh and alive, and the people involved are enthusiastic, motivated, and productive. Looking behind the scenes, you find a leader who has qualities not found in tthe average person. He is a leader who excels.

Excellence

The first necessary quality in a leader who stands out is the spirit of excellence. He who strives for excellence will not be counted among the also-rans. But where does a person start in an effort to develop this attribute? How does a leader develop a spirit of excellence in a day when almost anything can be passed off as good enough? The answer: he must start with God Himself. He must consider the excellence of God and His attributes.

• *God's name is excellent.* "O Lord our Lord, how excellent is Thy name in all the earth! who hast set Thy glory above the heavens" (Ps. 8:1). "Let them praise the name of the Lord: for

His name alone is excellent; His glory is above the earth and heaven" (Ps. 148:13).

• *God's loving-kindness is excellent.* "How excellent is Thy loving-kindness, O God! therefore the children of men put their trust under the shadow of Thy wings" (Ps. 36:7).

• *God's greatness is excellent.* "Praise ye the Lord. Praise God in His sanctuary; praise Him in the firmament of His power" (Ps. 150:1).

• *God's salvation is excellent.* "Behold, God is my salvation; I will trust, and not be afraid: for the Lord Jehovah is my strength and my song; He also is become my salvation. Therefore with joy shall ye draw water out of the wells of salvation. And in that day shall ye say, 'Praise the Lord, call upon His name, declare His doings among the people, make mention that His name is exalted. Sing unto the Lord; for He hath done excellent things: this is known in all the earth' " (Isa. 12:2-5).

• *God's work is excellent.* "Give ear, O ye heavens, and I will speak; and hear, O earth, the words of my mouth . . . Because I will publish the name of the Lord: ascribe ye greatness unto our God. He is the Rock, His work is perfect: for all His ways are judgment: a God of truth and without iniquity, just and right is He" (Deut. 32:1-4).

• *God's way is excellent.* "As for God, His way is perfect: the word of the Lord is tried: He is a buckler to all them that trust in Him" (2 Sam. 22:31).

• *God's will is excellent.* "I beseech you therefore, brethren, by the mercies of God, that ye present your bodies a living sacrifice, holy, acceptable unto God, which is your reasonable service. And be not conformed to this world: but be ye transformed by the renewing of your mind, that ye may prove what is that good, and acceptable, and perfect, will of God" (Rom. 12:1-2).

Many other Scriptures also carry this theme. Note this carefully: a spirit of excellence in the life of a leader is a reflection of one of God's attributes. Too often Christians misunderstand this emphasis and associate it with fleshly effort and worldly ambitions. This is not so! Throughout the Scriptures we observe a constant emphasis on emulating God, being like Him.

David, toward the end of his life, made an interesting statement regarding the work of building the temple. "David said, 'Solomon my son is young and tender, and the house that is to be builded for the Lord must be exceeding magnifical, of fame and of glory throughout all countries: I will therefore now make preparation for it.' So David prepared abundantly before his death" (1 Chron. 22:5). Why did David feel so strongly about this and insist that the temple of God must be "exceedingly magnificent"? Because it reflected on the name of God, which is excellent in all the earth. This Scripture is a pointed reminder to the leader: if what you are doing is in the name of the Lord, make certain it reflects well on that name, that it is exceedingly magnificent.

The desire to do things with excellence is Christlike. It was said of Him, "He hath done all things well" (Mark 7:37). It is amazing to observe Christian leaders who emulate the compassion and love of Christ but completely miss this aspect of His character. I have seen sermon topics such as "Becoming More Like Jesus" in church bulletins so sloppily done they were a scandal and a disgrace. What a paradox!

I remember hearing John Crawford, presently representing The Navigators in New Zealand, tell about a construction job he was heading up in Los Angeles. The Navigators were constructing their new office building. It was almost completed and the crew was working on the back door that led into the alley. Dawson Trotman was due to return to Los Angeles shortly, and they were rushing to complete the job before he came home.

Trotman, the founder of The Navigators, was a man of exacting standards, so the work on the office had been done with that in mind. However, since there was hardly any traffic by the back door, and because they were in a hurry they finished it with half-way measures.

When Dawson returned he was enthusiastic about the way the office looked. He inspected everything and was full of compliments for the workers. Then he saw the back door. "John," he said, "we'll have to change that door."

"But, Daws, it only leads to the alley."

"Yes, I know, John," Daws answered, "but when we do things for the Lord, the back door must look just as good as the front."

I've often thought about that statement and wondered what motivated Daws to think that way. I suppose it's because he knew that God sees the back door in the same way He sees the front, even if man does not.

Dawson's secretaries tell of his exacting standards on how envelopes and letters had to look. Pastors around the country wrote to tell them how they had been challenged by the appearance of the letters from The Navigators. Some even mentioned the care with which they now prepared the church bulletins, greatly raising the standards of their appearance.

During summer conferences at Glen Eyrie, the international headquarters of The Navigators, I have sometimes asked people at the end of a busy week: "What was the biggest challenge you've had from your time here?" More often than not the answers have been:

"The diligence with which the young men mop these floors!" / "I was amazed at the way you keep the grounds." / "I was really challenged by the way those guys washed windows in the castle."

The influence of one man who insisted on things being done with excellence remains long after his death.

In the parable of the talents, the good servant is commended; the slothful servant is not only denounced, but his sloth is equated with wickedness (see Matt. 25:14-30). Recall also Paul's admonition, "Not slothful in business; fervent in spirit; serving the Lord" (Rom. 12:11).

God works in our lives in at least seven ways to bring about the spirit of excellence.

1. *By helping us realize our own weakness.* "And He said unto me, 'My grace is sufficient for thee: for *My strength is made perfect in weakness.*' Most gladly therefore will I rather glory in my infirmities, that the power of Christ may rest upon me" (2 Cor. 12:9).

2. *Through the prayers of others.* "Epaphras, who is one of you, a servant of Christ, saluteth you, always laboring fervently for you in prayers, *that ye may stand perfect and complete* in all the will of God" (Col. 4:12).

3. *Through someone sharing the Word with us.* "Night and day praying exceedingly that we might see your face, and *might perfect that which is lacking* in your faith" (1 Thes. 3:10).

4. *As we study the Bible for ourselves.* "All Scripture is given by inspiration of God, and is profitable for doctrine, for reproof, for correction, for instruction in righteousness: That the man of God *may be perfect, throughly furnished* unto all good works" (2 Tim. 3:16-17).

5. *Through suffering.* "But the God of all grace, who hath called us unto His eternal glory by Christ Jesus, after that ye have suffered a while, *make you perfect, stablish, strengthen, settle you*" (1 Peter 5:10).

6. *By giving us a hunger for holiness.* "Having therefore these promises, dearly beloved, let us cleanse ourselves from all filthiness of the flesh and spirit, *perfecting holiness* in the fear of God" (2 Cor. 7:1).

7. *Through a desire to have the fruit of our lives brought to perfection.* "And that which fell among thorns are they, which, when they have heard, go forth, and are choked with cares and riches and pleasures of this life, and *bring no fruit to perfection*" (Luke 8:14).

Some words of caution need to be sounded at this point. First, we need to examine our motivation. Excellence for its own sake is not our standard, but excellence for Christ's sake.

I have been married for 27 years to a wonderful woman. To my shame I must admit that at times I have forgotten our wedding anniversary. But when I've remembered it, I have brought my wife roses. Now how would it be if I marched into our home on June 21 and said, "Well, here they are! More roses! For years I have brought these things to you, and here is another bunch. Right on time. I feel it is my duty to do this, so here they are! Enjoy them!"

How would that go over? Like a cement zeppelin! If I bring roses simply because on anniversaries I bring roses, they mean little.

Now let's say it's one of those years when I fail to remember. Three days later it hits me like a helicopter blade that our anniversary has come and gone. I hurry down to the florist and get a bunch of roses and walk into the house with them held behind my back. I go up to Virginia and say, "Well, Sweetheart, I'm sure you know what I did. It baffles me how you can manage to put up with the likes of me, but I'm glad you do. Sweetheart, I want to give you these roses, tell you I love you madly, and ask your forgiveness. Can you find it in your heart to forgive me one more time?"

Let me ask you, how does that go over? Like a new bike at Christmas! Why? I wasn't on time, I had forgotten, I had blown it. In the first instance I was right on time doing the right thing, but it didn't count. In the second instance I had failed, but all turned out well. Why? Motivation made the difference.

The second thing to bear in mind is that there has been only one Person who has ever lived *who did all things well.* That Person of course was Jesus. With that in mind, read carefully Hebrews 13:20-21: "Now the God of peace, that brought again from the dead our Lord Jesus, that Great Shepherd of the sheep, through the blood of the everlasting covenant, make you perfect in every good work to do His will, working in you that which is wellpleasing in His sight, through Jesus Christ; to whom be glory for ever and ever." The writer sets quite a standard—"make you perfect in every good work to do His will!"

How can anybody possibly achieve that? "Through Jesus Christ!" Through Jesus Christ, the only One who has ever done all things well, every moment of every hour of every day of His life. So my only hope of achieving a Christlike standard of excellence is to completely relax in the arms of Jesus and let Him live His life through me. No amount of sweat and strain can accomplish it. No amount of self-effort and high resolves. Only "through Jesus Christ" can this be obtained.

He who is the Author and Finisher of our faith waits to take over our frustrations and failures and turn them into joyful accomplishments that bring glory to the Lord. The One who still does all things well is waiting to "make you perfect in every good work . . . working in you that which is wellpleasing" to God.

Initiative

The second characteristic of the successful leader is initiative. He doesn't wait for things to happen; he helps make things happen. He's out at the point of the action. That's one reason some people shy away from leadership responsibilities. They know that "he who would lead the band must face the music." One of the necessary traits of the leader is that he be willing to do just that.

The Scriptures abound with examples of people who took the initiative in accomplishing God's purposes in their day. For example, David chose Joab to be his general for this very reason. "And David said, 'Whosoever smiteth the Jebusites first shall be chief and captain.' So Joab the son of Zeruiah went first up, and was chief" (1 Chron. 11:6). Isaiah also stepped out from the ranks to become a voice for God in his generation. "I heard the voice of the Lord saying, 'Whom shall I send and who will go for Us?' Then said I, 'Here am I; send me' " (Isa. 6:8).

It is obvious that initiative is a basic quality of leadership. Suppose there is a giant snowstorm the night of the midweek prayer meeting. A few hardy souls make it to church, open the doors, turn on the lights, and wait for the pastor to arrive. Unknown to them, however, the pastor is stalled in a snow drift and is working furiously to get his car moving again. He borrows a shovel and digs out. He hails a couple of guys to give him a push but all to no avail. His car doesn't budge, and the time is getting later and later.

Meanwhile, back at the church the people are wondering what's happened to their pastor and are sitting around waiting to begin. Finally one of them stands up and suggests that they sing a hymn or two while they wait. He announces the page and begins to lead the song. In this example it doesn't matter whether the man has ever led music or not; he has become the leader. He may be skillful or not. He may or may not know anything about how to go about it. By the simple act of exercising a little initiative in standing to his feet, he has become the leader. He may do a good job or a bad one, but regardless of his performance he is the man in charge. Initiative is one of the major responsibilities of leadership.

Of course, every Christian should take initiative in presenting himself to God for service. Bible characters who never became known particularly as leaders were richly blessed and used of God simply because they served spontaneously.

Rebekah became the wife of Isaac and "the mother of millions" because she took the initiative in serving Abraham's steward. She volunteered to draw water from the well, not only for him but for his camels, a big chore; and this act marked her as God's chosen bride for Isaac (see Gen. 24:14-21).

A small boy became the focal point of a great miracle because he stepped forward and offered his lunch to help feed a hungry multitude (see John 6:9-11).

But the greatest example in Scripture is God Himself. "Simeon hath declared how God at the first did visit the Gentiles to take out of them a people for His name" (Acts 15:14). Left to themselves the Gentiles would not have come to Him, so the Lord took the initiative. "God commendeth His love toward us, in that, while we were yet sinners, Christ died for us" (Rom. 5:8). To take the initiative is a God-like characteristic.

The leader must be alert to exercise initiative in many ways. One, already suggested, is in the area of serving. The Apostle Paul demonstrates this vividly. The ship in which he was traveling to Rome was wrecked on the island of Melita. The islanders were hospitable to the survivors, "for they kindled a fire, and re-

ceived us every one, because of the present rain, and because of
the cold. And when Paul had gathered a bundle of sticks and
laid them on the fire, there came a viper out of the heat, and
fastened on his hand" (Acts 28:2-3). Here is Paul, an older man,
gathering firewood for the others. No doubt he was as tired as the
rest, but he took the initiative to serve the others, as Christ would
have done when He walked the earth.

The leader of a teen-age Bible class in our city, a young man
named Mark Sulcer, gave of himself unreservedly. He hauled the
teens around in his car to various church and school functions. He
straightened up after them following the Bible classes. Mark was
always available to them day or night. I could see that these kids
had not met anyone quite like him before and were much impressed.

When Christmas came two teens got their heads together and
planned to get Mark a surprise present. Without telling anyone
about it, they went to a shopping center and made all the arrange-
ments. When Christmas Eve came they gave Mark his present.
He opened the box to find a silver trophy cup with the engrav-
ing: "To the world's second greatest servant."

Mark's life and example rubbed off on his followers, and they
are showing signs of growth in this area. His initiative is paying
dividends.

A second way of exercising initiative is to take the first step
toward reconciliation. Two Scriptures give clear guidance in his
area. "Therefore if thou bring thy gift to the altar, and there re-
memberest that thy brother hath aught against thee: leave there
thy gift before the altar, and go thy way; first be reconciled to
thy brother, and then come and offer thy gift" (Matt. 5:23-24).
"Moreover if thy brother shall trespass against thee, go and tell
him his fault between thee and him alone: if he shall hear thee,
thou hast gained thy brother" (Matt. 18:15). If you have offended a brother and the Lord brings this to mind, you should take
the initiative to go and ask for his forgiveness. If, on the other
hand, a person has offended you, you should still take the initiative to go to him and talk it over and get it straightened out. In
either situation, *it's your move first!*

This, of course, is one of the hardest things in the world to do.
It is especially difficult for a leader. Several missionaries have
told me of struggles they have had with this while on the field.
Pride was the chief obstacle. When they were willing to swallow

their pride and take the initiative, the Lord brought joy, deliverance, and blessing into the respective situations.

One of the devil's tactics is to make the leader think that if he humbles himself and goes to a member of the group to ask for forgiveness or get something straightened out, the person will look down on him. Nothing could be farther from the truth. It is in that very act that the leader is at his best, and the other person knows it. Usually the leader will win a loyal follower, a good friend, and faithful helper in the work.

A third area in which to exercise initiative is that of seeking knowledge. "Counsel in the heart of man is like deep water; but a man of understanding will draw it out" (Prov. 20:5). The job of the leader is complex and he cannot be expected to know all there is to know about everything. Therefore he should seek out knowledgeable men and learn from them.

Again, pride often gets in the way. I recall an incident in my own life when this happened. I had been transferred from a ministry in the field to a responsibility at headquarters. I had not spent a great deal of time at our home base prior to this, so was not too sure about what went on. I found myself on committees discussing things about which I knew very little. But I was hesitant to admit this and ask questions. I thought they expected me to be knowledgeable. I was convinced that to start asking questions would reveal how ignorant I was. So I continued in my ignorance.

From time to time for example I would be invited to sit with the finance committee. Months passed before I discovered that when they referred to the I.R.S. they were talking about the income tax people! You can imagine how valuable I must have been to this committee. Had I forgotten my pride and taken the initiative to ask some questions, I might have been of some service. The leader cannot afford to behave as I did. He must actively seek the information he needs to carry on his work properly. He must ask questions. He must be willing to learn from others.

Initiative is defined as *the spirit needed to originate action.* How does a leader acquire that spirit? How does one become the sort of person who originates actions? The most productive thing he can do is *to train himself to think ahead.* A leader has been described as a person who sees more than others see, who sees farther than others see, and who sees before others do.

If one trains himself to think ahead, it will have two positive effects on his work. *First, it will help keep him out of trouble.* He will avoid snares and pitfalls down the road. He can ask himself, "If we do this, what is likely to happen? In turn, what will that lead to? When that takes place, will it lead to this result? Do we want that result? If not, let's not even start in that direction." *Second, by thinking ahead the leader can set goals* for himself and his group. He can then think through the best ways to achieve those goals and begin to initiate actions along those lines.

All of this presupposes that the leader is in vital daily fellowship with the Lord through the Word and prayer (see chap. 2). Otherwise he may be led by his own understanding or set up plans using the wisdom of the world as his guide. The leader must remember that truth is found in Jesus Christ. Secular management books or textbooks on leadership are helpful, but our basic resource is God. "Because the foolishness of God is wiser than men; and the weakness of God is stronger than men" (1 Cor. 1:25).

Creativity

The third reason some leaders excel is that they are creative. They are not afraid to try new and different things. When you look at the lives of the apostles you do not find the monotony and stiffness that characterizes so many lives today. This difference may be traced to the very nature of God as contrasted to the nature of man.

To explain, God is a God of variety and order, while man thrives on conformity and disorder. Man struggles to conform. Go into any city, look at the houses made during the same period of time, and they all look alike. Man fights to be like his fellowman in speech, dress, and that which he buys. Music can be identified with the various decades; it has a sameness about it.

How refreshing it is, by contrast, to see the Lord at work. He loves variety. I am astounded by the diversity in a zoo. The alligator, giraffe, and elephant reveal God's love for variety. The flowers and birds and trees teach the same truth. Scientists tell us that no two snowflakes are alike. When we reflect on all of this, isn't it sad that our work for God is so different from the work done by Him. The same old dull bland programs are carried on year after year. Creativity, generally, is sadly lacking.

The creativity of the Lord was demonstrated to me in an astounding, remarkable, and humorous way recently. My wife and

I were visiting Soviet Russia. As we made ready to depart, we were required to sign a paper declaring we were taking no Russian rubles out of the country. We were allowed to keep the small change for souvenirs, but it was a crime, subject to severe punishment, to try to leave the country with Russian paper money. We exchanged the rubles we had for American dollars, and signed the paper. We cleared the passport check and waited in the lounge for the plane to take us to Helsinki.

Our plane was eventually called and we lined up to be searched. The first man through was a very large, loud American tourist. After they had checked his carry-on luggage, he passed the metal detector and the bell rang. He emptied his pockets and tried again. The bell rang. He took off his belt and tried again. Bong! By this time he was becoming quite amused by it all and started to laugh. He could be heard all over the waiting room. This happened over and over again with the same result and he laughed louder and louder.

Here were about 40 of us waiting to have our hand bags, purses, and carry-on luggage searched, and a fat, loud American, stripped down to a pair of tight-fitting pants and T-shirt was going round and round through the metal detector and continually ringing the gong. There was absolutely no reason for the bell to ring, but it did. The guard grew more agitated and the crowd became more hilarious all the time. We were at an impasse.

Through all this commotion, my wife was standing next in line waiting to have her purse searched, not knowing that at the bottom were eight Russian rubles! She had missed them when we exchanged the money. She was all set to be caught and convicted of a serious crime in Russia. But the show went on. The man kept ringing the bell while he roared with laughter. The plane departure was delayed, but the crowd didn't mind. They had never seen anything like it. It was a carnival. But it was not funny to the guard. One of the gods of the Soviet Union is their technology, and their god was being mocked by a crowd of American tourists.

Finally the guard, angry and frustrated, screamed, "Go!" My wife innocently walked to the plane carrying her forbidden rubles. When we arrived in Helsinki she discovered the money and we were shocked. Then we knew why the bell had rung for no apparent reason. The Lord looked down, saw two of his foolish children in a jam, and got them out of it. Once again He displayed His innovative, creative nature. Creativity is part of His being.

Sometime ago I was sitting in the office of the president of an international Christian organization. We were discussing the work of God around the world and he showed me a letter he had just received from one of his field men. The letter was full of news and contained many encouraging reports of God's blessing on the work. But one sentence was highly disturbing to the leader. It said, "We've been following the same program for the past five years and it's still producing."

The president looked up at me and said, "If they have been following that same program for the last five years, it's obvious they shouldn't be. There must be a better way!"

I've given a lot of thought to that statement, and I'm convinced he is right. There *must* be a better way! Surely we haven't hit on the best possible approach to reaching the lost or discipling believers. Surely there is room for improvement. Surely God can reveal changes and new approaches that will reap a greater harvest for His kingdom.

The creativity of four nameless men who brought their friend to Jesus has long been a challenge to me. "Many were gathered together, insomuch that there was no room to receive them . . . And they came unto Him bringing one sick of the palsy, which was borne of four. And when they could not come nigh unto Him for the press, they uncovered the roof where He was: and when they had broken it up, they let down the bed wherein the sick of the palsy lay. When Jesus saw their faith, He said unto the sick of the palsy, 'Son, thy sins be forgiven thee' " (Mark 2:2-5).

Here were four men who had a problem. They had a friend they wanted to bring to Jesus but found it to be impossible. The record says, "They could not come nigh unto Him." No way. They could have said, "Sorry, friend. We tried but we just can't do it." But they didn't. Their compassion and love for the man and their zeal to get him to Jesus led to a bold and creative plan. They would tear a hole in the roof and let him down from the top. Can't you just see the reaction? "You can't do that! That's never been done before! You will disrupt the service. Someone is liable to get hurt by a falling tile." But they did it and the Holy Spirit faithfully recorded it for our instruction.

How do you gain a creative spirit? One way is to keep yourself in the proper frame of mind. Constantly be on the lookout for a better way. Train yourself to think, "If it works, it will soon be obsolete." Maintain an open and probing mind. Pray for the boldness and courage it will take to try something new when God reveals it to you.

But the main thing is to live in constant, close, intimate fellowship with Jesus Christ. He is creative. "For by Him were all things created, that are in heaven, and that are in earth, visible and invisible, whether they be thrones, or dominions, or principalities, or powers: all things were created by Him, and for Him" (Col. 1:16). Everything in the invisible spiritual world was created by Jesus Christ. Everything in the visible physical world was created by Him. That's why the Bible speaks of Christ as the One by whom God "made the worlds" (Heb. 1:2). Worlds. Plural: visible and invisible. Do you want to be a creative person? Then you must invest much time in fellowship with the One who is the most creative Person in the universe.

When He walked the earth as a doer-teacher, Jesus astounded those who met Him. What He *did* was different. They said, "We never saw it on this fashion." What He *said* was different. They were astonished at His doctrine. They said, "Never men spake like this Man" (John 7:46). Some saw it and complained that He lived contrary to their longstanding traditions. You and I look back and say, "Thank God He did!"

By the same token you and I must be willing to break new ground and step out of the established mold. When the Lord sees leaders in His work with this spirit and desire, He can place His hand on their lives and say as He did of old, "Behold, I will do a new thing!"

Three things, then, we must seek from the Lord. One is a sense of excellence. The means for achieving excellence, once we've made it our standard, is to relax in the arms of Jesus and let Him live His life through us. He's the only One who "did all things well." The second is initiative. Here again the Lord Himself is our greatest example. To learn from Him as we seek to do His work is the most productive path we can follow. Third is a creative spirit. Again, open-hearted fellowship with Jesus Himself is the best means of seeing creativity developed in our lives by the Spirit of God.

6

How to
Make an Impact

His father was a mess. When you look at the record of the father, King Ahaz, you begin to wonder if all he did was sit around thinking up new ways to sin and lead the people astray. For 16 years he wallowed in the mire of wickedness. He made molten images to pagan gods and burnt his children in the fire after the way of the heathen. He closed the doors of the house of God and set up idolatrous altars on every corner in Jerusalem. After he had blown it for 16 years, he died.

As was the custom of the time, his son reigned in his stead. When Hezekiah took over the kingdom he was 25 years old. He had seen what his father's sins and corruption had done, and he wanted no part of it. He was determined to change things and call the nation back to God. When we consider the mess he inherited we might conclude that very little could be done in one man's lifetime, but we would be wrong. In a very short time the situation was completely reversed. "So there was great joy in Jerusalem: for since the time of Solomon, the son of David, king of Israel, there was not the like in Jerusalem" (2 Chron. 30:26).

It's an amazing story. Hezekiah made an impact for God that was truly marvelous. As you study his life, you see that it is characterized by a few basic principles. Three are readily identifiable.

Wholeheartedness
The first principle in making an impact for God is wholeheartedness. "And in every work that he began in the service of the house

of God, and in the law, and in the commandments, to seek his God, he did it with all his heart, and prospered" (2 Chron. 31:21).

The Apostle Paul exhorts us along similar lines, "Whatsoever ye do, do it heartily, as to the Lord, and not unto men" (Col. 3:23). Solomon put it this way, "Whatsoever thy hand findeth to do, do it with thy might; for there is no work, nor device, nor knowledge, nor wisdom in the grave, whither thou goest" (Ecc. 9:10). As we read these passages we can see that God wants men who are eager and zealous. But what do we find to be the spirit of the age in which we live? Are we frequently exhorted to wholeheartedness? Hardly. Almost daily we hear people telling us, "Take it easy" / "Don't work too hard" / "Don't overdo it." The dangerous thing is that this lack of wholeheartedness can be picked up by the Christian leader. When it is, it spells mediocrity and failure in his work.

My high school ideal was a senior nicknamed "H-ball." He excelled in sports and was a good student. I would imitate his walk and mannerisms. I learned to dribble a basketball like he did and shoot the same way. He pitched on the baseball team, and I copied everything he did, including the way he wore his cap. I was determined to become the pitcher when he graduated.

The year following his graduation I showed up for baseball try-outs. The coach came over to me and asked if I'd like to play. "Would I? Coach, I'll give it all I've got. I want to play so bad I can feel it."

In every way I knew, I tried to communicate to him my eagerness and determination. He was pleased and told me to suit up and see what I could do. I made the team. In fact, I became the pitcher.

What do you think would have happened if I had told the coach, "Oh, I don't know. I've been giving it some thought, but it's no big deal. Maybe I'll try out for the team, but it's not all that exciting to me." Why, the coach wouldn't have given me a second look. That would have been the end of my baseball career.

Do you think God has lower standards than my high school baseball coach? Not at all! God is looking for people who make wholehearted commitments to Him and to His service. The soft, slovenly, half-hearted spirit of the age is not His standard. But it is hard to keep a biblical standard in an undisciplined age. Your standard of performance must be high.

In my first year of Christian service in the Midwest I met a young man named Johnny Sackett. We began to fellowship together in the Word and prayer, and the Lord knit our hearts together. Johnny began to show great promise in the work of Christ. One day he asked me if he could join our team. I explained to him what was involved, and he was eager to be part of our gang. He was a great colaborer, full of dedication and enthusiasm.

For a number of months things went great. One weekend we planned a team activity of witnessing on the campus of Iowa State University. When it came time to drive over to the school, I noticed Johnny was missing. When I inquired about it, one of the guys told me he had decided not to go. When I asked if he was under pressure of studies or didn't feel good or had some responsibilities with his parents, I was told that he just decided not to go.

We went without Johnny and had a fruitful time. We met quite a few students who were eager to talk about the Lord, and some committed their lives to Him. We returned full of joy and thanksgiving to God.

On Monday I borrowed a friend's VW and drove down to see Johnny. After we had talked a while, I asked if he had understood the standards the team had set for itself. He said yes and he was happy to be a part. I told him that because I enjoyed having him on the team I was sorry he had chosen not to work with us any more. He was shocked and asked what I meant. I reminded him that one of our standards involved being available when we had a ministry together. He began to sob. After he regained his composure, he got out of the car and went to his room.

I prayed for Johnny daily for about two weeks and then got a letter from him. He thanked me for making it mean something to be part of the ministry and then gave me 13 reasons why he should be included. I immediately telephoned him and joyfully welcomed him back. He became one of our most productive men then and has served the Lord on two continents since. The problem had been that he had no idea that I really meant it when I talked about standards of commitment and wholeheartedness. Sympathy for him could have let the incident slide, but compassion would not.

When Jesus said, "If any man will come after Me, let him deny himself and take up his cross daily, and follow Me," He meant it.

Frankly, as I look back over a 20-year perspective, I know I would handle the situation differently today. I would be quicker to show the tenderness and gentleness of Christ. But the principle remains inviolate.

My drill instructor in Marine boot camp insisted on high standards of performance, not because he was trying to be mean to me but because he knew I was going to war and he had to instill habits into me that could save my life. He was not doing me harm. He was doing me good. And when I was under fire, and death and destruction were all around me, I was grateful for all that I had learned. By the same token, the leader must manifest the spirit of wholeheartedness so that those who follow him will have their hearts in the work. Had Hezekiah displayed anything less than wholehearted involvement, the nation could not have turned from its sins in such a remarkable fashion. It was his leadership that showed the way and set the tone for the behavior of others.

I was in Minneapolis working out on the weights with a friend of mine named Bill Cole. Another fellow joined us for awhile, and as he was leaving the gym I had 185 pounds over my head in a bench press. He looked at me and said, "Take it easy!" Had I taken it easy at that moment I would have killed myself! Naturally he wasn't intending that; it was just his way of saying good-bye. But I've thought about that often. Even when it doesn't fit, and would be the death of the person if he followed that advice, we still say, "Take it easy!" Frankly, I don't need that sort of exhortation. I am prone to do that without any outside help. My undisciplined, slovenly, lazy nature tells me to do that all the time. What I need is to be challenged to hit it with all I've got.

The leader must consider the following fact. He is not only building for the present but also for the future. If his heart is lukewarm, what will the future hold? What will the people he has trained be like? Will their hearts burn with wholehearted zeal for God? Not if his heart is lukewarm, for only fire kindles fire. When Jesus cleansed the temple his actions reminded the apostles of the Old Testament Scripture, "The zeal of Thine house hath eaten Me up" (John 2:17; see Ps. 119:139). Both passages speak of being consumed with zeal for God. When was the last time you reminded anyone of a Scripture that spoke of being devoured with holy zeal? Is an eager and ardent spirit as out of date as the horse and buggy? Are cheerleaders at high school sports events the only ones left in our society who enter into their jobs with zeal and gusto? A truly Christlike leader will demonstrate the same fire and intensity that Jesus displayed.

Wholeheartedness and zeal are the outgrowths of a love that burns in the leader's heart. From there it spreads to the hearts and lives of others, who catch the flame of that spirit. Some feel that the leader should play it "cool" lest he frighten off some people. This is not so. If the leader plays a man's game, then men will come to play. The first commandment is still in the book: "Hear, O Israel; the Lord our God is one Lord: and thou shalt love the Lord thy God with *all* thy heart, and with *all* thy soul, and with *all* thy mind, and with *all* thy strength" (Mark 12:29-30).

Singlemindedness
The second thing to observe in the life of Hezekiah was his singlemindedness. He got right at the main job and stuck with it. "He, in the first year of his reign, in the first month, opened the doors of the house of the Lord, and repaired them. And he brought in the priests and the Levites, and gathered them together into the east street, and said unto them, 'Hear me, ye Levites, sanctify now yourselves, and sanctify the house of the Lord God of your fathers, and carry forth the filthiness out of the Holy Place'" (2 Chron. 29:3-5). He was not sidetracked, either by overwhelming odds, ridicule, or opposition.

Three biblical writers give us reasons for singlemindedness. Peter says, "But the day of the Lord will come as a thief in the night; in the which the heavens shall pass away with a great noise, and the elements shall melt with fervent heat, the earth also and the works that are therein shall be burned up" (2 Peter 3:10). *Everything in this world is temporal and transient.* Two things transcend this world and will last throughout eternity: the Word of God and the souls of men. When the leader gives himself to these, he is locked on eternal values. The things of the world clamor for his attention, but he keeps his eyes single to the things that last.

A second reason for being singleminded is suggested by the words of James, "Whereas ye know not what shall be on the morrow, for what is your life? It is even a vapor, that appeareth for a little time, and then vanisheth away" (James 4:14). *Life is too short to be wasted.* When a person sees this truth, it helps him remain on track despite the incessant bombardment of the world seeking to turn him aside, to get his eyes off Jesus. The Word of God tells us where to look: "Wherefore, seeing we also are compassed about with so great a cloud of witnesses, let us lay aside every weight and the sin which doth so easily beset us, and let us run with patience the race that is set before us, *looking unto Jesus,* the Author and Finisher of our faith; who for the joy that was set before Him endured the cross, despising the shame, and is set down at the right hand of the throne of God" (Heb. 12:1-2).

The third reason for singlemindedness is stated by Paul, "Therefore my beloved brethren, be ye steadfast, unmoveable, always abounding in the work of the Lord, forasmuch as ye know that *your labor is not in vain* in the Lord" (1 Cor. 15:58). When we are following the straight and narrow path with our eyes on Jesus, we have the assurance that what we are doing is worth something. What a thrill it is for the leader to know that while multitudes are throwing their lives away in worthless activities, his service for Christ counts for eternity.

The Bible is filled with examples of men who were singleminded in their walk with God. Moses is typical. "By faith Moses, when he was come to years, refused to be called the son of Pharaoh's daughter; choosing rather to suffer affliction with the people of God, than to enoy the pleasures of sin for a season; esteeming the reproach of Christ greater riches than the treasures in Egypt; for he had respect unto the recompence of the reward" (Heb. 11:24-26).

The Apostle Paul sounds the same note, "Brethren, I count not myself to have apprehended, but this one thing I do, forgetting those things which are behind, and reaching forth unto those things which are before, I press toward the mark for the prize of the high calling of God in Christ Jesus" (Phil. 3:13-14).

But the greatest example is Jesus Himself. "And it came to pass, when the time was come that He should be received up, He steadfastly set His face to go to Jerusalem" (Luke 9:51). His men saw this and were amazed. "And they were in the way going up to Jerusalem; and Jesus went before them: and they were amazed; and as they followed, they were afraid. And He took again the 12 and began to tell them what things should happen unto Him" (Mark 10:32). Why were they amazed? Because He knew exactly what awaited Him and marched forward without flinching. He said, "Behold, we go up to Jerusalem; and the Son of man shall be delivered unto the chief priests, and unto the scribes; and they shall condemn Him to death, and shall deliver Him to the Gentiles" (Mark 10:33).

Something in Jesus' countenance caused the 12 to feel uneasy. They were afraid of what lay before them and were awed by the courage of their Leader. Jesus Christ went with unfaltering steps straight to the cross. He knew His mission and He was set to fulfill it. So it must be with us. The world nags at us to become ensnared with this or encumbered with that, but the Word of God calls us to strip down, lay aside every weight, and press toward the mark. Singlemindedness is not easy, but it is necessary.

When Billy Graham preached Dawson Trotman's funeral sermon, he spoke of Daws' singlemindedness. He told us, "Here was a man who did not say, 'These 40 things I dabble at,' but 'This one thing I do.' "

A man can destroy his life in one of three ways. The first is to give in to his lazy slothful nature and do nothing. I've seen young men go down that road. They buy a guitar, put on a pair of cutoffs, go to the beaches of sunny California, and waste their lives lying around frying in their own fat.

The second way to destroy your life is to give yourself to a goal, work hard, and discover at the end that you gave yourself to the wrong goal. I have known many who have done this. Some have poured out their story in bitter regret and tears.

The third way is what Dr. Graham was talking about. Become a dabbler and never really do anything.

Joshua was warned about dabbling, "Only be thou strong and very courageous, that thou mayest observe to do according to all the law which Moses My servant commanded thee: *turn not from it to the right hand or to the left,* that thou mayest prosper whithersoever thou goest" (Josh. 1:7). This is not a warning against walking down the wrong path, but against turning first to one side and then another.

I've watched men like that. They start out well, but something comes along that grabs their fancy and they are sidetracked. They finally see the folly of their ways and turn back to the path, only to be sidetracked again by something else farther down the road. A pitiful thing! Good men, with good hearts, going nowhere. Why? Easily diverted. The singlemindedness of Moses or Paul or Christ Himself is not a part of their lives.

Someone complains, "That's tough to do." Of course it's tough!

The Apostle Paul said, "I *press* toward the mark." He did not say, "I float toward the mark, I glide toward the mark, I slip and slide toward the mark, or I drift toward the mark." He said *press,* and that always presupposes opposition. The world will lure you and the devil will fight you, but if you run the race looking unto Jesus He will enable you to finish well.

Paul's testimony vividly illustrates this: "But none of these things move me, neither count I my life dear unto myself, so that I might finish my course with joy, and the ministry which I have received of the Lord Jesus to testify the Gospel of the grace of God" (Acts 20:24). He speaks of "my course." The greatest joy in life is to know that you are in the perfect will of God, doing what He wants in the way He wants it done.

The warriors of Zebulun challenge us in this regard: "Of Zebulun, such as went forth to battle, expert in war, with all instruments of war, 50,000, which could keep rank: they were not of double heart" (1 Chron. 12:33). Here were men that went into battle, trained, equipped, disciplined, and singleminded.

Each of us has a course to follow, a mission to accomplish, a goal to attain. "Say to Archippus, 'Take heed to the ministry which thou hast received in the Lord, that thou fulfill it' " (Col. 4:17).

I recall an incident in my life that determined my destiny. My wife and I had met the Lord through reading the Bible. We did not have many people around us who could give us deep spiritual counsel, but we both became convinced we should follow the Lord with singleness of purpose. A pastor, the Rev. Arlan Halverson of Harlan, Iowa, told us about a school in Minneapolis where we could learn the Word of God. We were new Christians and eager to grow, so we determined to go to that school and give our lives completely to Christ's service. I had a good job at the time and when I began to tell my co-workers about what I was planning to do I received nothing but static. They called it foolishness—fanaticism. Throwing away a good job with high pay and security was madness. But we knew what we must do.

I quit my job and prepared to leave Council Bluffs, Iowa, for Northwestern College. We sold some of our possessions, gave away most of the rest, and were free to go. We put our clothing and a few household items in small boxes, loaded them on a child's coaster wagon and headed for the train station. Virginia pulled the wagon and I pushed, and we launched out on a road of high adventure. We determined we would not only not look back, but we would not even look to the right or to the left. We would keep our eyes on Jesus and follow Him wherever He led. Twenty-five years have passed and we have faced opposition and trials, but He continues to show us the way.

Today the Lord is looking for people who care nothing for the empty praise or temporal pleasures of this world. He is seeking men and women who care that the world needs Christ and who are eager to follow Him with singlemindedness and purpose. The testimony of Paul is an encouragement: "For I am now ready to be offered, and the time of my departure is at hand. I have fought a good fight, I have finished my course, I have kept the faith; henceforth there is laid up for me a crown of righteousness, which the Lord, the righteous Judge, shall give me at that day: and not to me only, but unto all them also that love His appearing" (2 Tim. 4:6-8).

A Fighting Spirit

In addition to his wholehearted and singleminded approach to the job, Hezekiah also demonstrated a remarkable fighting spirit. In spite of unbelievable odds he pressed ahead with enthusiasm and faith. His messengers were mocked by some as they went from place to place. "So the posts passed from city to city through the country of Ephraim and Manasseh even unto Zebulun: but they laughed them to scorn, and mocked them" (2 Chron. 30:10). Did it slow down his work? Not at all. "And thus did Hezekiah throughout all Judah, and wrought that which was good and right and truth before the Lord his God" (2 Chron. 31:20).

This is the basic spirit we see in the lives of God's leaders throughout the Bible. Paul's testimony is: "Of the Jews five times received I 40 stripes save one; thrice was I beaten with rods; once was I stoned; thrice I suffered shipwreck; a night and a day I have been in the deep; in journeyings often; in perils of waters, in perils of robbers, in perils by my own countrymen, in perils by the heathen, in perils in the city, in perils in the wilderness, in perils in the sea, in perils among false brethren; in weariness and painfulness, in watchings often, in hunger and thirst, in fastings often, in cold and nakedness. Beside those things that are without, that which cometh upon me daily, the care of all the churches" (2 Cor. 11:24-28).

What was Paul's attitude through all his difficulties? "For unto you it is given in the behalf of Christ, not only to believe on Him, but also to suffer for His sake" (Phil. 1:29).

Nehemiah faced continual opposition from the enemy. "It came to pass, that when Sanballat and Tobiah, and the Arabians, and the Ammonites, and the Ashdodites, heard that the walls of Jerusalem were made up, and that the breaches began to be stopped, then they were very wroth, and conspired all of them together to come and to fight against Jerusalem and to hinder it" (Neh. 4:7-8). His fighting spirit is revealed in his response. "Nevertheless we made our prayer unto our God, and set a watch against them day and night, because of them" (Neh. 4:9).

Time and again the opposition mounted an attack to keep Nehemiah from accomplishing his objective, and every time he prevailed. "Sanballat and Geshem sent unto me, saying, 'Come, let us meet together in some one of the villages in the plain of Ono.' But they thought to do me mischief. And I sent messengers unto them, saying, 'I am doing a great work, so that I cannot come down: why should the work cease, whilst I leave it, and come down to you?' They sent unto me four times after this sort; and I answered them after the same manner" (Neh. 6:2-4).

The Apostle Paul calls our attention to the life of a soldier, an athlete, and a farmer. "Thou therefore endure hardness, as a good soldier of Jesus Christ. No man that warreth entangleth himself with the affairs of this life; that he may please Him who hath chosen him to be a soldier. And if a man also strive for masteries, yet is he not crowned, except he strive lawfully. The husbandman that laboreth must be first partaker of the fruits" (2 Tim. 2:3-6).

The mark of a good soldier is that he worries the enemy. The enemies of the cross of Christ became nervous when Paul was around. Because of his work in Ephesus, Demetrius the silversmith was convinced all was lost (see Acts 19:23-28). Paul was opposed by the leaders of false religions and the demons of hell, but he was undaunted. He truly demonstrated the mark of a good soldier.

An athlete competes with opponents, of course, but quite often his main competition is with himself. He has to overcome his own doubts and fears, his sloth, and the desire to pamper himself. The Apostle Paul tells of the battles in his own life. "And every man that striveth for the mastery is temperate in all things. Now they do it to obtain a corruptible crown; but we an incorruptible.

I therefore so run, not as uncertainly; so fight I, not as one that beateth the air: but I keep under my body, and bring it into subjection; lest that by any means, when I have preached to others, I myself should be a castaway" (1 Cor. 9:25-27). The leader will constantly face problems and difficulties from others but often his main battles are with himself.

The farmer faces droughts, floods, and pestilence of every variety. I recall how one of our farms in Iowa suffered a tremendous hailstorm a few years ago. The corn had been about six feet high but was so badly hit you could hardly tell it was a cornfield. The storm was so violent it knocked the steeple off the church and broke countless windows. A seed company in Shenandoah, Iowa heard of our plight and sent some help. They brought a truckload of soybeans and told us if we would get them in the ground we would have feed for the livestock for the winter.

We didn't know much about soybeans in those days, but we knew it was too late to replant the corn, so we gave it a try. Sure enough we were able to get enough feed for the animals to make it through the winter. The storm was a tremendous blow to my brother who was running the farm, but to this day I can see him rolling up his sleeves and fighting back. I'm sure it would have been easy for him to throw up his hands and cry, "What's the use?" But he didn't. He demonstrated the true fighting spirit.

After Waldron Scott and his family went to the Middle East as missionaries in the late 1950s, everything went wrong. Finances were so low they couldn't afford furniture, so Joan made a slipcover for their steamer trunk and they sat on it in the living room. The water heater blew up and burned her quite severely. Through a series of strange circumstances Scotty was thrown in jail. They literally were pressed to their knees. Only the fighting spirit of this family and their faith in the promises of God kept them going. Today there are young men and women throughout the Middle East whose lives were touched with the Gospel of Christ that Scotty and Joan subsequently shared with them. These Christians are strong, rugged soldiers of the cross who saw a clear example of a true soldier of Christ. Out of impossible circumstances came a harvest for the kingdom.

This is what made the servants of Christ in the New Testament church so outstanding. They had the fighting spirit of committed warriors for God. They were "men that have hazarded their lives for the name of our Lord Jesus Christ" (Acts 15:26). Does this characterize the leadership of the Christian enterprise today? In some cases, yes, but all too often we look at a person's intellectual powers or his educational achievements as the apex of all good. I heard a man praised on one occasion because he had a 10,000-volume library! Obviously there is nothing wrong with owning or reading good books. We are to love the Lord our God with all our *minds*. But the leader must never stop there. It is not a brilliant mind but a fighting spirit that will keep him going when all semblance of order has crumbled around him.

Early in his Christian life the Apostle Paul was shown what he was to suffer. "The Lord said unto [Ananias], 'Go thy way, for [Paul] is a chosen vessel unto Me, to bear My name before the Gentiles, and kings, and the children of Israel: For I will show him how great things he must suffer for My name sake'" (Acts 9:15-16). He was shown the prize he was to gain, but he was also shown the price. He knew the cost of discipleship. Later he said, "But God forbid that I should glory, save in the cross of our Lord Jesus Christ, by whom the world is crucified unto me, and I unto the world. . . . From henceforth let no man trouble me: for I bear in my body the marks of the Lord Jesus" (Gal. 6:14, 17). When the apostle wanted to refute his detractors, he showed them the scars on his back. The early Christians faced dangers, whips, and lions. They were heroes in the true sense of the term. We face push buttons, television, and foam rubber. May God give us the same fortitude and faith men of God have always shown.

These three things, then, are essential to making an impact as a leader. We must be wholehearted, singleminded, and have a fighting spirit. Programs may continue without these, but the leader whose life is to be used of God to produce much lasting fruit will see that he has all three.

7

Setting the Stage
for Success

Plan a Good Beginning

Beginning is difficult. You're new to the job; the people around you are watching to see what you will do; and you may feel uneasy and insecure. Some people in that situation cover their feelings of inadequacy by beginning to "bull their way around." This normally upsets people, and you spend the next few months trying to get out of the hole.

Lorne Sanny, the president of The Navigators, tells about a lesson he learned while he was running a servicemen's center in Southern California. When he first took the job, he would stand in front of the center and hand out invitation cards to servicemen passing by and ask them to come in. Most walked right on by. Then he hit on an idea. He would go up the street a few blocks and fall in step with some guys who were walking along. He would get in a conversation with one or two of them, and when they got to the center he'd ask if they wanted to stop in for a cup of coffee and talk for a while. More often than not some of them would take him up on it.

So it is when we begin a new job. We must not try to stop people and try to get them to abruptly change directions. We must fall in step with them for a while and walk along in the direction they are heading. Then, after we have established a little communication with them, we can suggest a change of direction. That way we are more likely to have a hearing and get a positive response.

The Bible gives us some guidance in this matter in a rather strange setting. Saul is not known as a model of spiritual leadership. His failings and shortcomings have often been noted by men in the pulpit and by authors of books. But I am challenged by the good beginning this man had as a leader—and by the wisdom he showed. We can learn an important lesson from his example.

Samuel had called the people together unto the Lord to Mizpeh. From the tribe of Benjamin, Saul was taken. "And when they sought him he could not be found. Therefore they inquired of the Lord further, if the man should yet come thither. And the Lord answered, 'Behold, he hath hid himself among the stuff' " (1 Sam. 10:21-22). It is obvious that Saul was not seeking the job or trying to put himself forward. He displayed a humble spirit.

Even after Saul had been chosen king in the sight of all the people, he quietly went home. He displayed great restraint and control over his own spirit when some of the people mocked him. "But the children of Belial said, 'How shall this man save us?' And they despised him, and brought him no presents. But he held his peace" (1 Sam. 10:27).

Sometime later a situation arose that required a bold step of leadership. The Ammonites wanted to put out the right eyes and make servants of the people of Javesh, or else they would make war on them. To submit would have rendered the people of Javesh helpless to protect themselves. In warfare a large shield was held in the left hand and a sword in the right. The shield blocked much of the vision of the left eye; hence to lose the right eye was to be severely handicapped in battle. They could still tend sheep and plant crops, but their ability to defend themselves would be lost.

Meanwhile, Saul had returned to his farm and was tending his sheep. To me that fact speaks volumes about the man. Here was a man who had been anointed king of Israel, but he was not immediately trying to throw his weight around. He was back with the sheep. No doubt he was waiting for some situation to arise in which he could be of genuine help to the people. He was waiting until his new responsibility matched a real need. In such a case the people would appreciate his leadership and be glad to follow him.

The Ammonite threat was that kind of situation. When Saul heard of the plight of his countrymen, he sent out a call to muster the troops to come to the aid of those in need. The people came with one consent. In the ensuing battle, Saul's forces devastated the Ammonites.

After the people were delivered from their oppressors, they were so solidly committed to Saul that they thought to make retaliation against the men who had mocked him earlier. "Who is he that said, 'Shall Saul reign over us?' Bring the men, that we may put them to death" (1 Sam. 11:12).

Saul immediately stepped in. "And Saul said, 'There shall not a man be put to death this day: for today the Lord hath wrought salvation in Israel' " (1 Sam. 11:13).

Notice, Saul did not call attention to himself by saying, "I have done this or that," but he gave all the glory to God for what had been accomplished.

At this point Saul had Israel's full allegiance and confidence. The people were ready to follow him. He was off to a good start. His call from God was evident to all. His actions and bold step of faith had wrought deliverance for the downtrodden.

This is a great lesson for anyone who has been called to lead. Don't be in a hurry to make a lot of changes. Don't be in a hurry to show anybody who's boss. If you have some changes you would like to set in motion, first just get people thinking in that direction.

This is another lesson I have learned from Lorne Sanny. He usually sees things before the rest of us Navigators, so he will begin to plant seed thoughts. He will toss out an idea or ask a question that will get us thinking along certain lines. Then when the plan is actually proposed, some of us have been thinking about it so long that we think it's our idea!

Changes can be made. New ideas will be adopted. New directions can be instituted. But it often takes time. People resist change. So fall in step with them, walk with them in their direction for a while, and then gradually ease them into new and more productive paths.

Do Your Homework

After you're off to a good beginning, there is another thing you must practice. Do your homework. Become known as the guy that has the answers. When you have a project to propose or a suggestion to make, know the facts. Know what it will cost. Know how long it will take. Be able to explain why it is a good idea.

The Book of Nehemiah is often studied by leaders. Nehemiah— the ancient governor of Jerusalem—is frequently called the effective executive. Here was a man who knew how to get things done. Let's take a look at him in action to see what we can learn about doing our homework.

Nehemiah had been living in the comfort of the palace, holding the prestigious position of cupbearer to the king. One day he learned of the desperate plight of his countrymen in Jerusalem: "And they said unto me, 'The remnant that are left of the captivity there in the province are in great affliction and reproach: the wall of Jerusalem also is broken down, and the gates thereof are burned with fire' " (Neh. 1:3).

The Lord burdened Nehemiah's heart with this news, and it sent him to his knees in prayer (see v. 4). One day some time later he was going about his duties but still burdened in his heart for the situation in Jerusalem. The king noticed his depressed mood and asked him, "Why is thy countenance sad, seeing thou art not sick? this is nothing else but sorrow of heart" (Neh. 2:2).

Upon then hearing of Nehemiah's concern, the king asked, "For what dost thou make request?" (v. 4) The first thing Nehemiah did was to pray to the Lord, and then he gave the king his answer. And his answer is classic. He had done his homework. If he hadn't he would have stumbled around and quite possibly blown his opportunity.

Nehemiah said, " 'If it please the king, and if thy servant have found favor in thy sight, that thou wouldest send me unto Judah, unto the city of my fathers' sepulchres, that I may build it' "

"And the king said unto me, (the queen also sitting by him), 'For how long shall thy journey be? and when wilt thou return?' So it pleased the king to send me; and I set him a time." "Moreover I said unto the king, 'If it please the king, let letters be given me to the governors beyond the river, that they may convey me over till I come into Judah; and a letter unto Asaph the keeper of the king's forest, that he may give me timber to make beams for the gates of the palace which appertained to the house, and for the wall of the city, and for the house that I shall enter into.' And the king granted me, according to the good hand of my God upon me" (vv. 5-8).

I hope you will catch the significance of that little scene. From what we saw earlier, it is obvious that Nehemiah had been on his knees before God and had spent much time in prayer over the problem. But he didn't stop there. He had thought through what he would need to do the job. It is obvious he thought in terms of an answer to his prayers. And he was ready when the answer came.

Imagine what would have happened when the king asked him what he needed, if he had said, "Well, O King, I haven't thought much about it. I'd kind of like to go out there myself, with your permission, of course, and I suppose I'd need some favors from you. Could I go and think about it for a few days?"

But no! Nehemiah had done his homework and knew exactly what the project demanded: letters to the governors beyond the river; a letter to the keeper of the king's forest; soldiers and some horsemen. He had done his homework.

Plan the Work

When you are given a responsibility, one of the first things you should do is spend time discovering exactly what your new mission is. Let me suggest that it generally breaks down into two distinct but related goals. One is to do something through the work to advance the cause of Christ. The other is to see each member of your group have his or her life deepened in the Lord and become a more productive member of the Body of Christ.

Let's discuss first how to accomplish your objective of forwarding the cause of Christ through the work. This can take the form of setting a goal to evangelize the area where your church is located, getting a Gospel tract to every home in the city, and so on. You must then break this goal down into workable units and find qualified people to fill the key spots. Give them the authority to take action and check on them from time to time to make sure they are at the main job.

In our work we follow a four-step plan called **POLE**: Plan, Organize, Lead, and Evaluate. This can all sound cold and technical unless you think of it in an actual setting. Let's say for instance that some Saturday you and your group have decided to spend the morning cleaning up around the church. That is your goal. It's a nice day in early spring and there is much to be done after a rather hard winter.

You decide to meet at 9:00 A.M. and work until noon. You ask members of the group to bring rakes, buckets, cleaning rags, paint brushes, brooms, mops, and whatever else you will need to get the job done.

You assemble, have a time of prayer, and commit your work to the Lord. Then you break the job down into workable units. Joe takes a couple of guys and begins to work on the lawn. Pete and Hank start washing the windows. You and four men tackle the basement, cleaning and doing a little touch-up here and there with the paint brush.

Joe comes in about an hour later and says the lawn work is going well—raking, trimming the bushes, and so on, and wonders if they should go down to the nursery and get some flowers to set out. You go out and see how it is coming. It is evident to you immediately that if they start that additional project they will not get the main job wrapped up by noon, namely, the clean-up project. So, you suggest they stay at the original idea and then, if they get finished in time, take on the additional job of planting a few flowers. Joe is content with that suggestion and returns to the clean up.

Now there are a couple of other ways you might have handled Joe. One would have been to read him off for getting sidetracked and tell him to follow orders and do what he was told. This would have accomplished two things: One, you would have taken the heart out of Joe for the job. Secondly, you would have stifled any idea-sharing on Joe's part in the future. Later, when you were trying to figure the best way to evangelize the neighborhood, Joe would have been afraid to speak up for fear of being blasted out of the saddle.

Along about 11:00 A.M. you make the rounds to see how the projects are coming. It is evident to you that Pete and Hank are not going to get all the windows washed and that your own crew is going to finish ahead of time. So you pull two guys from your own crew and get them helping the window washers. At noon you assemble and take a look at what got done. Mission accomplished. The tools are gathered and cleaned. You have a word of prayer together to thank the Lord for the good morning, hop in your cars, and head for home.

Any job will fit into that framework. You must think it through and make a plan. Then you must organize it so that every member of the group knows what his job is and who he reports to. Then the leader must lead. He himself must set the example—roll up his sleeves and get into the action. A periodic evaluation may lead to a midcourse correction. At the finish of the job it is good to sit down and evaluate the whole project to see where things could have been improved. This leads to better planning for the future.

Now let's take two of those points and look at them a bit more carefully: selection of key people and your own involvement as a leader.

First, selection. The best painter is not always the best man to head the paint crew. The one who heads the project should be able to paint, but in addition he should be the sort of person who inspires others to do their best and keeps the spirit of the group high.

Before Jesus chose His 12 apostles, He prayed all night (see Luke 6:12-13). The Apostle Paul told Timothy: "And the things that thou hast heard of me among many witnesses, the same commit thou to faithful men, who shall be able to teach others also" (2 Tim. 2:2). He was to look for faithful men with some ability to teach.

One thing I look for is when a man begins to call the activity of the group "our work." It is evidence that he has gotten involved. When a new person joins a group, he is somewhat a spectator—watching what is going on. After some time he may begin to participate a bit more. Your goal is to lead him from spectator to participant to one who is involved. It is from that last group that you want to look for your key people to head projects.

Make sure of your man before you give him a key task. I've learned this the hard way. It is generally easier to get a person into a place of leadership than it is to get him out. Paul said, "Lay hands suddenly on no man" (1 Tim. 5:22). This refers to ordaining leaders and it's good advice. Later on we'll take a look at some of the *qualities* to look for in selecting key people to help get a job done through the group.

Now about your own involvement in the work you lead. Are you to roll up your sleeves and pitch in with the rest of the group? Absolutely! The power of example cannot be overstated. Peter told the leaders of the Early Church: "Feed the flock of God which is among you, taking the oversight thereof, not by constraint, but willingly; not for filthy lucre, but of a ready mind; neither as being lords over God's heritage, but being ensamples to the flock" (1 Peter 5:2-3). We too should be "examples to," not "lords over." Christians have a Lord already.

Be involved in doing the work you expect to lead others to do. I once agreed to teach a Sunday School class for the summer. One of my goals was to increase the attendance of the class, which had been running at about 20 college-age kids who came fairly regularly.

For the first two or three Sundays I encouraged them to bring someone to class the following week. No one did so I began to make it a matter of prayer. During one of my prayer times the

Lord revealed to me why no one was bringing anyone else to class: I wasn't.

I began to think how I could meet some college age kids to bring to class. One Sunday I noticed a group of young servicemen lounging around the park next to the church, and the Lord gave me an idea.

The next Sunday my wife and I and our two kids went to Sunday School a half hour early. We strolled over to the park and invited a few servicemen to come to Sunday School with us. Now there is nothing more harmless looking than a man and wife and two kids. So some of them came. They had nothing else to do. When it came time to introduce the visitors I'd introduce the three or four guys who came with me.

This went on for a couple of Sundays, and then one of the class members came and inquired where I was getting all these guys. I told him of my pre-Sunday School activity. He was interested and asked if he could come along. We met the next Sunday, split up to different parts of the park, and got quite a few guys. Some other members of the class caught the idea and began to do the same thing.

By the end of summer, scores of guys had met the Lord, and our class was averaging around 180 per week. I learned a simple lesson. My job was to teach the class and to provide leadership for them. It's summarized in Proverbs 4:11: "I have *taught* thee in the way of wisdom; I have *led* thee in right paths."

In addition to seeing a mission accomplished through your group, there must also be a deep work done in the lives of each member of the group. The real test of your leadership is whether or not other leaders are developed as you lead the way. The development of Christlike character in the people for whom you are responsible is one of your prime objectives. Because of the importance of this point, it is discussed at length in chapter 11.

These have been a few tips—often learned the hard way—on how to begin your job and carry it out. I trust they will prove valuable to you as you grow in true spiritual leadership.

8

How to Get More Done

It's a common problem. There's more to do than there is time to do it. The housewife, the worker, the boss, the student all face it. Projects to finish—tests to study for—reports overdue. The calendar and the clock: nag, nag, nag. If only I had more time.

Let me share a little secret with you that could change your life.

Do It Now

A simple idea is illustrated in the Book of Numbers in the Old Testament. We look in on the main character and what do we find? A busy man. Moses has been given the job of moving thousands of people out of slavery in Egypt across the burning sands of the Sinai to the promised Land. And they are a troublesome bunch—always doing something stupid and incurring the disfavor of the Lord. Time and again God's patience is put to the test. And Moses is forever trying to straighten things out. He is constantly endeavoring to get across lessons in faith and duty and obedience and courage and purity of life. He is the leader of God's training program in the wilderness.

The people continually complain about lack of food or water, or the lack of variety in their menu. They murmur against Moses himself. They say the real reason he led them out of Egypt is to kill them. Or he has married the wrong wife. Or all this talk about God is just Moses' means of making himself a big man. The problems seem endless. Moses has his hands full.

And then one day out of the clear blue sky the Lord drops more work on him. "And the Lord spake unto Moses . . . on the first day of the second month, in the second year after they were come out of the land of Egypt, saying, 'Take ye the sum of all the congregation. . . . From 20 years old and upward, all that are able to go forth to war in Israel: thou and Aaron shall number them by their armies' " (Num. 1:1-3).

Now, let's assume that Moses is human—like us. What would your reaction have been? Mine would have been something like: "Count everybody???!! Good grief, do You know how long that will take? I've got my hands full now! Look at all I'm doing: responsible for the physical and spiritual welfare of all these people —that alone keeps me going from morning til night—plus the fact that I *am* writing the Bible! I'm a busy man with more to do than there's time for as it is. And now I'm supposed to count everybody?"

Sound familiar? But hold on to your hat, and look at Moses' response: "And Moses and Aaron . . . assembled all the congregation together on the first day of the second month, and they declared their pedigrees after their families, by the house of their fathers, according to the number of the names, from 20 years old and upward, by their polls" (vv. 17-18).

Did you notice when the job was given? "On the first day of the second month." And when did Moses start the project? "On the first day of the second month." How about that! There's a tremendous secret we can express in three words: *do it now*. Especially if it is something that comes along while you're doing something important.

I was in Oakland, Calif. on my way to speak to a group of army men at Fort Ord. The chaplain had arranged for me to share the Gospel with them. After that I was to go to another part of town to speak at an "Andrew Dinner"—where some Christian men had invited their non-Christian friends to a pizza feed followed by a message. There was just one catch. In order for me to make both meetings, I'd have to miss supper. The schedule was that tight. Fine and dandy—no problem. But just as I was leaving the house a package came for me. It was a rather lengthy personnel form from headquarters that they needed right away. Bill already had the car started and in the driveway. What to do?

Take it with me and do it tomorrow? No time. Tomorrow we were heading for Hume Lake to visit a training program and it would take the full day.

I called down for Bill to turn off the engine. I sat down and filled out the form. It took quite a while but I got it done. I left it to be mailed, hopped in the car, and we made the meeting. Had I not done it then, I would have carried that thing around for days.

I am responsible for two categories of work: the kind I *like* to do and the kind I *have* to do. My tendency is to do what I like and leave until later what I have to do. The problem with that scheme is that the undone, unpleasant work is always pulling on my sleeve, reminding me it's there.

I really enjoy speaking to servicemen about the love of God as revealed in Jesus Christ. It's a thrill to speak at an Andrew Dinner and watch the men lead their friends to Christ during the fellowship time that follows. Filling out personnel forms? *Blah!* I *could* have waited—and when the long distance phone call came, I could have just given headquarters my schedule. They are reasonable people. They would probably have understood. But for the next week everytime I reached into my briefcase for my Bible—there would have been that packet of papers, leering at me. And so I took the time to "do it now" and hit the road with a released spirit.

As you read the record of Moses' life you don't get the idea that "paper shuffling" was his thing. But when God gave him a great long personnel form to fill out, rather than sit down and complain that he didn't have time—or that he was involved with something *really important*—or that "surely somebody else could take care of things like *that*"—he *did it now*.

You're probably thinking, "OK, fair enough. I can see how that would help in certain instances, but there's another problem. There's more to do than I can do by myself. I need some help."

Right. This situation faces us all from time to time. The Sunday School superintendent needs teachers. The pastor needs workers. The missionary needs personnel for his staff to help in the physical end of things. The sponsors of the young people's department need drivers of automobiles. The deacons need help in distributing food to the needy. The ladies on the committee for the annual church dinner need help. This problem is universal. It comes to all of us at one time or another.

Trust God for the Help You Need
As in so many situations in life, the Christian has an advantage here that the non-Christian knows nothing about. Again, this is

illustrated in the life of one of the busiest men in the Old Testament, Aaron.

When his appointment came I suppose Aaron's reaction was about what ours would have been. Thankfulness, exhilaration, excitement, a sense of unworthiness, and gratitude for the privilege of being involved in such an important work. "And thou shalt bring Aaron and his sons unto the door of the tabernacle of the congregation, and wash them with water. And thou shalt put upon Aaron the holy garments, and anoint him, and sanctify him; that he may minister unto Me in the priest's office" (Ex. 40:12-13).

At first I suppose the tremendous significance of the job and the importance of the task occupied most of Aaron's working thoughts. What a position to hold! And think of the honor of having his sons serve beside him! Of all men he was truly blessed of God.

But as they got into the work, another train of thought must have been set in motion: *This is really a busy job in more ways than one! All these people continually bringing their offerings. All these cattle to be sacrificed to the Lord. And the tremendous job to keep the area cleaned up! Burning certain parts, saving certain parts, burying certain parts—work, work, work! What I need is help.*

No doubt the thought remained with Aaron for some time, and intensified when the two oldest sons, Nadab and Abihu, died before the Lord when they offered strange fire. Now he was left with only two sons, and the two youngest at that! The task that seemed great before must have seemed mountainous now. How in the world could he get all his work done?

The New Testament says, "But my God shall supply all your need according to His riches in glory by Christ Jesus" (Phil. 4:19). Aaron's need was help. And I'm sure he had no idea how he was going to get it. But God knew. He had a plan all along. He had 22,000 Levites waiting in the wings ready to go to work.

"And the Lord spake unto Moses, saying, 'Bring the tribe of Levi near, and present them before Aaron the priest, that they may minister unto him'" (Num. 3:5-6).

So now, in addition to two young sons, he had 22,000 men between the ages of 30 and 50 to help. Isn't that just like God! When God meets a need, He *meets* it!

A number of Scriptures tell us of the relationship the Lord intended Aaron to have with these men. Two of these contain vital lessons for us as we are given people to help us in our God-given tasks.

Numbers 8:11, 19: "And Aaron shall offer the Levites before the Lord for an offering of the children of Israel, that they may execute the service of the Lord. . . . And I have given the Levites as a gift to Aaron and to his sons from among the children of Israel, to do the service of the children of Israel in the tabernacle of the congregation."

The clauses, "Aaron shall offer the Levites before the Lord," and "I have given the Levites as a gift to Aaron," teach an important truth. Here the Levites were offered by Aaron to God and then God gave them back. This is to be true not only of helpers in our tasks but of our homes, our professions, our children, and our very lives.

Numbers 18:6: "And I, behold, I have taken your brethren the Levites from among the children of Israel: to you they are given as a gift for the Lord, to do the service of the tabernacle of the congregation."

Do you see the truth revealed in the words, "to you they are given as a gift for the Lord"? These helpers are a gift *from* the Lord *for* the Lord. Not for you but for God. And if He sees fit to use them in another capacity, in a new job, rejoice! You can't outgive God. Notice, too, that helpers in our tasks are gifts from God.

So, the lesson in all this is faith. Trust the Lord. He has promised to supply and He will. But as in every other aspect of life, you must exercise faith. Believe God. And trust Him to provide the *right kind* of help.

In Aaron's case, God provided men between the ages of 30 and 50 years of age. Here were men with good judgment and stability. When Moses was called upon to number the people, it was all those "from 20 years old and upward, all that were able to go forth to war. . . . But the Levites after the tribe of their fathers were not numbered among them" (Num. 1:45, 47). The Levites were called to a *spiritual* warfare.

Why were the Levites recruited to their tasks at the age of 30, while the soldier was recruited at age 20? Note a New Testament parallel. Qualifications for church officers include: "Not a novice, lest being lifted up with pride he fall into the condemnation of the devil" (1 Tim. 3:6), and "Let these also first be proved; then let them use the office of a deacon, being found blameless" (1

Tim. 3:10). The person engaged in spiritual work must not be a novice and he must first be proved.

By the way, the Levites quit at age 50—probably so they wouldn't run down at the end of their service! God gave Aaron tested, proven men who were alive and active to help him in his work and spiritual warfare.

Focus on Objectives, Not Obstacles

Want to get more done? Make your first rule "do it now." Second, trust God to supply the held you need. And there is a third thing. It has to do with the focus of our attention, or the way we look at things. Somehow we seem to be wired to think negatively. It is so easy to focus on all the problems involved in a task. People rather commonly expect the worst. Example: someone receives a telegram late at night.

"You open it."

"No, you open it."

They both expect it to contain bad news.

The phone rings in the night. What's your first thought—positive or negative?

Negative attitudes can carry over in our outlook toward a task we're involved in. It can make us problem-centered rather than goal-centered. We tend to look at the difficulties. We get all hung up on the means whereby a thing can be done.

Moses fell into this trap. The people had been eating manna and they began to complain that they had no flesh to eat. "And the mixed multitude that was among them fell a lusting: and the children of Israel also wept again, and said, 'Who shall give us flesh to eat? We remember the fish, which we did eat in Egypt freely; the cucumbers, and the melons, and the leeks, and the onions, and the garlic: but now our soul is dried away: there is nothing at all, beside this manna, before our eyes" (Num. 11:4-6).

Moses began to complain to the Lord regarding the burden of the job. "Wherefore hast Thou afflicted Thy servant? and wherefore have I not found favor in Thy sight, that Thou layest the burden of all this people upon me? I am not able to bear all this people alone, because it is too heavy for me" (Num. 11:11, 14).

The first thing the Lord did was provide some help for Moses. "And the Lord said unto Moses, 'Gather unto Me 70 men of the elders of Israel, whom thou knowest to be the elders of the people . . . and I will take of the spirit which is upon thee, and will put it upon them; and they shall bear the burden of the people with thee, that thou bear it not thyself alone" (Num. 11:16-17).

Then the Lord promised that there would be flesh to eat—a change of diet. And it would be in abundance (see Num. 11:18-20).

Moses couldn't figure it out. How on earth could God find enough meat to feed all these people? "And Moses said, 'The people, among whom I am, are 600,000 footmen, and Thou hast said, "I will give them flesh, that they may eat a whole month." Shall the flocks and the herds be slain for them, to suffice them? or shall all the fish of the sea be gathered together for them, to suffice them?' " (Num. 11:21-22). He got involved in the means whereby this could be accomplished. Here was a God-given promise in plain Hebrew from the Creator of the universe, and Moses couldn't believe it. Why? Because he really didn't know God? No, he had spoken to God and knew His power. His problem was our problem. The details of the thing—the "means whereby"—the Lord would do it.

But God has His means. "And the Lord said unto Moses, 'Is the Lord's hand waxed short? thou shalt see now whether My word shall come to pass unto thee or not.' And there went forth a wind from the Lord, and brought quails from the sea, and let them fall by the camp, as it were a day's journey on this side, and as it were a day's journey on the other side, round about the camp, and as it were two cubits high upon the face of the earth" (Num. 11:23, 31).

Another illustration of human doubt about God's supply is seen in the disciples' reaction to the Lord's concern for the physical welfare of the people who were following Him. "In those days the multitude being very great, and having nothing to eat, Jesus called His disciples unto Him, and saith unto them, 'I have compassion on the multitude, because they have now been with Me three days, and have nothing to eat'. . . . And His disciples answered Him, 'From whence can a man satisfy these men with bread here in the wilderness?' " (Mark 8:1-4) But Jesus did it. He fed them with seven loaves and a few small fishes.

By contrast, consider the case of the women who had it on their hearts to anoint the body of their crucified Lord. "And very early in the morning the first day of the week, they came unto the sepulchre at the rising of the sun. And they said among themselves, 'Who shall roll us away the stone from the door of the sepulchre?' And when they looked, they saw that the stone was rolled away: for it was very great" (Mark 16:2-4).

Their minds were not on the stone but on the objective. They had awakened with a desire to do something for the Lord and they were undeterred by obstacles. The fact of the stone—or the guards at the tomb—didn't cause them to turn back. And the difficulties vanished before them when they pressed ahead in faith with their eyes on the goal. I imagine most of us would have gotten about halfway there, realized the futility of the idea, and returned to a warm bed for a few more hours of sleep.

Consider the 12 men sent by Moses to spy out the Promised Land. The report when they returned evidenced they were good intelligence agents. They had been diligent in their task. But it is interesting to note that their conclusions varied. Ten saw the difficulties—two saw the opportunities.

The report: "We came unto the land whither thou sentest us, and surely it floweth with milk and honey: and this is the fruit of it. Nevertheless the people be strong that dwell in the land, and the cities are walled, and very great" (Num. 13:27-28).

The conclusion of the two: "Let us go up at once, and possess it; for we are well able to overcome it" (Num. 13:30).

The conclusion of the ten: "We be not able to go up against the people, for they are stronger than we" (Num. 13:31).

Admittedly the people of the land were tough, and it was not going to be a Sunday School picnic. They were a fierce, immoral lot. The people of Caanan were not savages, but a highly developed race. But they were so vile and wicked that one historian says, "To destroy them was an act of mercy to the countries of the world. The happiness of the human race depended on it. If the Jews failed, the world would have been lost."

Caleb saw this as clearly as the rest, but note his words. He does not say "Let us go up and conquer it," but "Let us go up and possess it." Let us take possession of that which God is ready to give us.

Caleb saw the thing from God's perspective. Of course they were strong, but were they stronger than God? Was He not with Israel? Did He not go before them? Is anything too hard for Him? Of course their cities are walled. But are they walled to heaven? Can God not peek over? Are they too high for Him?

The Bible makes it clear what their problem was. "Yea, they despised the pleasant land, they believed not His word, but mur-

mured in their tents, and hearkened not unto the voice of the
Lord" (Ps. 106:24-25). *They didn't believe God.* They believed
what they saw—and got their eyes off God. Of course, there were
giants in the land, but when you think about it, there is only
about 14 inches difference between a giant and an average man.
Think how both must look to God.

I have a friend named Bob Boardman who lives in Tokyo.
Bob is a big, rugged ex-Marine who stands well over six feet tall.
When he walks down the streets of Tokyo he looks huge. But
if I were to go to the top of the Tokyo Tower and look down at
Bob and some of his friends, there wouldn't appear to be any
difference. If that's true, think how they must look from God's view-
point. So it all depends on one's perspective, one's point of view,
the way one looks at things. Do we see things from a problem-
centered perspective, or do we look at tasks with the promises of
God in mind?

But here's an interesting thing to consider. The facts of the
matter—the *real* facts were not at all as the men supposed. They
had supposed that the people looked upon them as grasshoppers.
"And there we saw the giants, the sons of Anak, which come of
the giants; and we were in our own sight as grasshoppers, and so
we were in their sight" (Num. 13:33).

But how did the people really view them? One of them, the
harlot Rahab said, "I know that the Lord hath given you the
land, and that your terror is fallen upon us, and that all the in-
habitants of the land faint because of you. For we have heard
how the Lord dried up the water of the Red Sea for you, when
ye came out of Egypt; and what ye did unto the two kings of
the Amorites, that were on the other side Jordan, Sihon and Og,
whom ye utterly destroyed. And as soon as we had heard these
things, our hearts did melt; neither did there remain any more
courage in any man, because of you: for the Lord your God, he is
God in heaven above, and in earth beneath" (Josh. 2:9-11).

Isn't that something! The people of the land were living in
terror, knowing they were doomed. They had heard of the Exodus
from Egypt, and the miracle at the Red Sea. Ever since, they had
dreaded the day when they would have to face these people whose
God fought for them so mightily and performed miracles and
wonders in their behalf. Their hearts melted and there was no
more courage left in any man.

Yet the people of God fainted for fear. They said in effect that

God was not able to fulfill His word. He had undertaken more than He could perform . . . bitten off more than He could chew.

They saw the obstacles, but were blind to God. There are those who think that the ability to see obstacles is a mark of maturity and insight. Really, this is the easiest thing to see. God wants men who see the way over the difficulty and give encouragement to the people.

What was the result of the report of the 10 spies? "And all the congregation lifted up their voice, and cried; and the people wept that night" (Num. 14:1). Discouragement inevitably resulted from believing these men and looking at circumstances rather than believing God. But Caleb and Joshua said, "The land, which we passed through to search it, is an exceeding good land. If the Lord delight in us, then He will bring us into this land, and give it us; a land which floweth with milk and honey. Only rebel not ye against the Lord, neither fear ye the people of the land; for they are bread for us: their defence is departed from them, and the Lord is with us: fear them not" (Num. 14:7-9).

Ultimately only Joshua and Caleb entered the Promised Land. The complainers, the doubters, the negative thinkers bleached their bones in the wilderness.

We must keep our eyes on our objectives not on the obstacles!

So, to review, when you undertake a task for God, remember three things:

1. Get right at it.
2. Trust God for the help you need.
3. Focus on objectives, not obstacles.

Of course, obstacles and difficulties can be very real and very serious. We can't expect them simply to go away just because we think positively. In the next chapter we will discuss how to resolve difficulties.

9

Resolving Difficulties

The skies are not always blue. Storms are as much a part of life as starlight. This fact can sometimes throw the leader into a quandary. He is serving the Lord, doing the will of God from the heart, but in the midst of it all he finds himself facing difficulties, dilemmas, and problems.

Difficulties for leaders usually come in two forms: problems with the group and problems in their own personal lives.

The Example of Moses
The Scriptures are filled with examples of men of God who ran into difficulties as they held positions of leadership. Moses was one. He ran into a problem at one point in his life because he tried to do everything himself. Some men are like that. Their philosophy is, "If you want a job done right, you've got to do it yourself."

An admirable feature about Moses in his situation was that he was personally involved with the people. He was not a nonworking supervisor. But his strength became his weakness. "And it came to pass on the morrow, that Moses sat to judge the people: and the people stood by Moses from the morning unto the evening" (Ex. 18:13). He was giving himself all day to a group of people who had recently tried to stone him to death. To serve and help people who appreciate what you are doing is relatively easy, but Moses was giving his time and energy to a crowd of ungrateful people, who were hateful, unappreciative, and thoughtless, and who had tried to take his life. Moses was a servant of God and was demonstrating a God-like spirit before them.

One day Moses' father-in-law saw what he was doing and asked him about it. "What is this thing that thou doest to the people? Why sittest thou thyself alone, and all the people stand by thee from morning unto even?" (Ex. 18:14)

Moses replied, "Because the people come unto me to inquire of God: when they have a matter, they come unto me; and I judge between one and another, and I do make them know the statutes of God, and His laws" (Ex. 18:15-16).

When Jethro heard this explanation, he gave Moses some sound advice, "The thing that thou doest is not good. Thou wilt surely wear away, both thou, and this people that is with thee: for this thing is too heavy for thee; thou art not able to perform it thyself alone. Hearken now unto my voice, I will give thee counsel, and God shall be with thee: be thou for the people to God-ward, that thou mayest bring the causes unto God: And thou shalt teach them ordinances and laws, and shalt show them the way wherein they must walk, and the work that they must do.

"Moreover thou shalt provide out of all people able men, such as fear God, men of truth, hating covetousness; and place such over them, to be rulers of thousands, and rulers of hundreds, rulers of fifties, and rulers of ten. And let them judge the people at all seasons: and it shall be, that every great matter they shall bring unto thee, but every small matter they shall judge: so shall it be easier for thyself, and they shall bear the burden with thee. If thou shalt do this thing, and God command thee so, then thou shalt be able to endure, and all this people shall also go to their place in peace" (Ex. 18:17-23).

One of the most amazing things in this record was the fact that Moses had the good sense to take that advice. Pride could have kept him from it. He could have said, "Who do you think you are, telling *me* what to do? Don't you know who I am? I am Moses, the man who has spoken to God Himself face to face. If I want advice I'll go right to the top and get it—I'll go to God Himself. I don't need one of my in-laws to come along and tell me what to do!" How easy it would have been for Moses to react like that! But he didn't! "So Moses hearkened to the voice of his father-in-law, and did all that he had said" (Ex. 18:24).

Now let's look more closely at the advice that got Moses out of his difficulties. Four things stand out.

1. *Moses' number one priority as a leader was to pray for the people under his charge.* "Be thou for the people to God-ward, that thou mayest bring their causes unto God." You therefore as a leader must make this your number one task. If you're a Sunday School teacher, pray for each member of your class by name. If you are the head of a department in the church, pray for those who report to you. If you are a pastor, elder, or deacon, pray for those who are under your care. "Epaphras, who is one of you, a servant of Christ, saluteth you, always laboring fervently for you in prayers, that ye may stand perfect and complete in all the will of God" (Col. 4:12). Praying for people will do a great deal to resolve problems or nip them in the bud.

2. *Moses was to teach the Word of God.* "Thou shalt teach them ordinances and laws." Whether publicly or privately, whether to the entire congregation or to one individual, the leader must help people learn what the Bible says and help them apply its truths to their everyday situations. People can't *do* the truth if they don't *know* the truth. Jesus prayed, "Sanctify them through Thy truth: Thy Word is truth" (John 17:17).

3. *Moses was to be a visible example to his people.* He had to show them "the *way wherein they must walk,* and the *work that they must do.*" It has been well said, "Tell them what, tell them why, and show them how."

Dawson Trotman, the founder of The Navigators, used to tell us, "Telling is not teaching; listening is not learning." The leader must show the people by example how to walk with God and how to work for God. People need help in learning how to live for Christ and how to serve Him. And people don't learn that from lectures and sermons. They must be shown. Like a dressmaker, they need a pattern to follow and the best pattern is the example that is set by the leader.

4. *Moses was to delegate his responsibilities.* Jethro finally got to the main issue. He told Moses to share the load with other men. "And let them judge the people at all seasons: and it shall be, that every great matter they shall bring unto thee, but every small matter they shall judge: so shall it be easier for thyself, and they shall bear the burden with thee." Moses must stop trying to do it all himself. He must share the load. But he must choose his associates carefully. They must have spiritual depth, be properly related to God, to their fellowmen, and to the world around them—"able men, such as fear God, men of truth, hating covetousness."

Getting the right person in the job is a blessing; getting the wrong person can be a curse. Remember that it is easier to get people into a position than to get them out. Careful selection of co-workers is a hallmark of a good leader. In the advice Jethro gave Moses, he taught him something of his personal priorities, the basics of his job, and the art of delegation. Any job, no matter how large and complex it is, can be broken down into workable and manageable units if we have the right people to place in charge.

Leaders-in-training

Those to whom responsibilities are delegated are actually leaders-in-training. They are colaborers. Three qualities must characterize the people you put in charge.

1. *Likemindedness* is a prerequisite to colaborship in the job. "For I have no man likeminded, who will naturally care for your state. For all seek their own, not the things which are Jesus Christ's" (Phil. 2:20-21). Your co-worker must agree with your goals and objectives. In fact, they must be his own. You in turn should be eager to allow him to carry them out in his own way, using his own methods and plans that are in line with the gifts and abilities that God has given him. The idea is this: agreement on goals; much latitude on methods and means.

Ezra and Nehemiah exemplify this principle. Each led a group of people from Babylon to Jerusalem. When Ezra started out, God gave him an idea as to how to proceed with his plan. "Then I proclaimed a fast there, at the river of Ahava, that we might afflict ourselves before our God, to seek of Him a right way for us, and for our little ones, and for all our substance. For I was ashamed to require of the king a band of soldiers and horsemen to help us against the enemy in the way: because we had spoken unto the king saying, 'The hand of our God is upon all them for good that seek Him; but His power and His wrath is against all them that forsake Him.' So we fasted and besought our God for this: and He was entreated of us" (Ezra 8:21-23). He was convinced that to go to the king and ask for help would be sin. He would fast and pray and launch out, trusting in God alone to take him and his people safely to Jerusalem.

Some years later Nehemiah felt led of God to undertake a similar project. His objective was the same: to take a group of people from Babylon to Jerusalem. But look at *his* approach! "Moreover I said unto the king, 'If it please the king, let letters be given me to the governors beyond the river, that they may convey me over till I come into Judah; and a letter unto Asaph the keeper of the king's forest, that he may give me timber to make beams for the gates of the palace which appertained to the house, and for the wall of the city, and for the house that I shall enter into.' And the king granted me, according to the good hand of my God upon me. Then I came to the governors beyond the river, and gave them the king's letters. Now the king had sent captains of the army and horsemen with me" (Neh. 2:7-9).

Ezra had felt it would be wrong for him to ask for human help. But not Nehemiah! He didn't want to set foot outside the city without letters to the governors and captains of the army and horsemen. He wanted all the help he could get. Now, who was right? The answer is simple: They were *both* right. God led one man to do it one way and the other to do it another way. But here is where we often get hung up. My method is this way and yours is that? Therefore you must be wrong! Not so. The objective must be clear, well-defined, and fixed. But methods may vary.

Notice how Ezra handled the problem of sin in the camp: "And when I heard this thing, I rent my garment and my mantle, and plucked off the hair of my head and of my beard, and sat down astonied [appalled]" (Ezra 9:3).

When Nehemiah found sin in the camp, he dealt with it in an entirely different way. "Then I testified against them, and said unto them, 'Why lodge ye about the wall? If you do so again, I will lay hands on you.' From that time forth came they no more on the sabbath. And I contended with them, and cursed them, and smote certain of them, and plucked off their hair and made them swear by God, saying, 'Ye shall not give your daughters unto their sons, nor take their daughters unto your sons, or for yourselves' " (Neh. 13:21, 25).

Again, they handled the problem differently. Ezra sat down and pulled out his hair. When Nehemiah discovered the people living in sin he pulled out theirs! Who was right? They were *both* right. The objective was to get rid of sin among the people. The methods of accomplishing the objective were completely different. So when you give a person a job, allow him the flexibility to exercise his God-given abilities as long as his approach is Christ-honoring and scriptural. But likemindedness is essential with regard to objectives.

2. *Maturity* is another prerequisite. Your colaborer must be

"not a novice, lest being lifted up with pride he fall into the condemnation of the devil" (1 Tim. 3:6). He must be able to handle the emotional impact of carrying responsibility. Two things happen to a person when he is given a load to carry in the program of the church. The responsibility makes him or breaks him.

I have watched young men and women grow and blossom, and I have seen them crash. Those who grew were those who accepted responsibility with a humble spirit and depended on the Lord for His sustaining grace and power. God used the added responsibility to cause them to exercise greater dependence on Him. It drove them to their knees and got them searching the Scriptures for guidance. They became stronger people, eventually able to carry a greater load.

On the other hand, I've watched people get a job and seen them set back in their walk with God. They became overbearing and dictatorial. Pride welled up in their lives and they suffered the consequences. God resisted them and they went nowhere.

It is important therefore for the leader to know his people and lead them step by step along the road of responsibility. "Lay hands suddenly on no man, neither be partaker of other men's sins: keep thyself pure" (1 Tim. 5:22). One of the best ways of doing this is to give the person a little responsibility first and see how it affects him. If he can handle it, he is ready for more. The leader who knows how to delegate and share the load with others is a blessing to his people. They will grow and develop and become spiritually qualified workers in a world where the laborers are few.

3. *Faithfulness* is the third necessary quality in a co-worker. The Bible says, "A faithful man, who can find?" (Prov. 20:6) Admittedly this person is a rare bird. It is difficult to find people you can count on fully. It seems that dependability is not one of the characteristics of our age. Maybe it never has been. "Help, Lord; for the godly man ceaseth; for the faithful fail from among the children of men" (Ps. 12:1).

Nevertheless, the leader will do well to wait for the faithful man to come along before he begins to share the load. Solomon gives us the reason. "Confidence in an unfaithful man in time of trouble is like a broken tooth, and a foot out of joint" (Prov. 25:19).

Two Scriptures I share with people in trying to help them build faithfulness into their lives express principles that Jesus taught His disciples. The first is the importance of *faithfulness in little things.* "He that is faithful in that which is least is faithful also in much: and he that is unjust in the least is unjust also in much" (Luke 16:10). The person who cannot see the importance of doing a small job faithfully will be the same person who fails in the larger tasks. You can tell much about a person by watching how he sets up chairs for a meeting or greets people as they arrive. It is quite easy to detect whether or not his heart is in it. The person who does a sloppy job in lining up the transportation for the class weekend retreat will do the same kind of job when he is asked to run the retreat.

The second principle is *faithfulness in working with others.* "And if ye have not been faithful in that which is another man's, who shall give you that which is your own?" (Luke 16:12) Some people just hate to be called on to help another person in his program. If it's not totally their own deal, they would just as soon not do it. Jesus taught that before you can have a responsibility that is your own you must learn to work with others and help them in their responsibilities.

That's why there is always room at the top. So few people are willing to learn how to handle ultimate responsibility by first fitting into the life and schedule and program of another. But the Scriptures are loaded with examples of this very thing. Joshua was "Moses' minister." Elisha was chosen as the one who "went after Elijah and ministered unto him." Each of these men became a great leader in his own right, but they first learned how to be faithful in that which was another man's.

The leader who has men and women who demonstrate these basic characteristics is blessed indeed. He will be able to delegate a good share of his workload to them and rejoice as the work goes forward in accomplishing the mission of the church.

Keeping Others Informed

The second area where the leader can hit some pretty rough snags is in assuming that people know what is going on. Or, in thinking everybody knows why the leader does things as he does. Moses ran into this problem: "For he supposed his brothers would have understood" (Acts 7:25). But they didn't. The leader soon learns to keep the lines of communication open. If he doesn't, it can lead to disaster.

This is vividly illustrated in the history of the children of Israel. The wars of conquest had been forgotten and the land enjoyed peace. "And the Lord gave unto Israel all the land which He sware to give unto their fathers; and they possessed it, and dwelt therein" (Josh. 21:43). The tribes that had their farms on the other side of the Jordan returned to their homes.

En route they built an altar by the Jordan River (Josh. 22:10). Then a strange and terrible thing happened. Hearing of the altar and imagining the worst, the rest of the children of Israel made plans to go to war against their brethren for idolatry!

Scripture describes the situation as follows: "And the children of Israel heard say, 'Behold, the children of Reuben and the children of Gad and the half tribe of Manasseh have built an altar over against the land of Canaan, in the borders of Jordan, at the passage of the children of Israel.' And when the children of Israel heard of it, the whole congregation of the children of Israel gathered themselves together at Shiloh, to go up to war against them" (Josh. 22:11-12). Imagine that!

After years of war—after years of being comrades-in-arms—they made plans for a civil war. Why? It was a simple misunderstanding which arose because the lines of communication were not open. The majority had only "heard" indirectly of the actions of the minority and knew nothing of the reasons behind their actions.

Happily, the majority sent a delegation across the river to determine the facts. The explanation was simple. The altar was "not for burnt offering, nor for sacrifice: but that it may be a witness between us and you and our generations after us, that we might do the service of the Lord before Him with our sacrifices, and with our peace offerings; that your children may not say to our children in time to come, ye have no part in the Lord' " (Josh. 22:26-27).

When the delegation heard the explanation they were satisfied and the matter was dropped (Josh. 22:30). Disaster was avoided. But note the pattern: hasty suspicion led to false accusations, which led to anger and division, which could have led to war. The leader must do what he can to prevent such situations by keeping people informed. Plans laid in secret have a way of bringing forth a negative response. An active endeavor to help people see what is being done and why it is being done will go a long way in stopping the rumor mill.

Most leaders agree that good communication is needed and at the same time tremendously difficult. The problem is compounded by the fact that in many cases the real source of dissension and division is the devil. One of his chief tools in disrupting the program of the church and stopping the thrust of the Gospel is to get Christians fighting among themselves. The leader must do everything he can to maintain a climate of love, peace, and harmony among his people. And that takes effort. "With all lowliness and meekness, with longsuffering, forbearing one another in love: endeavoring to keep the unity of the Spirit in the bond of peace" (Eph. 4:2-3).

A personal report to the people or an occasional newsletter helps. Asking people's advice and letting them in on decisions is very helpful in many ways. For one thing, the leader usually needs all the help he can get. Second, the people know they are in on the action and are making real contributions. This keeps morale high and misunderstandings to a minimum. This is a task the leader can't duck. He must face the responsibility of keeping information flowing and the lines of communication open. Though it's hard work and sometimes a pain in the neck, he'll be glad he did.

Doing Unpleasant Tasks
When a leader majors on those things that he enjoys doing and shirks tasks that are unpleasant to him, problems arise. There are many responsibilities involved in the leader's job, and he must be willing to fulfill them all. David is a classic example of this. David was a man who excelled in battle. He was a warrior, and a good one. He also ran the affairs of the people ably. He did not neglect the administrative duties of his office just because he preferred the excitement of leadership in battle.

Scripture describes the organization David established to run the country. "So David reigned over all Israel, and executed judgment and justice among all his people. And Joab the son of Zeruiah was over the host; and Jehoshaphat the Son of Ahilud, recorder. And Zadok the son of Ahitub, and Abimelech the son of Abiathar, were the priests; and Shavsha was scribe; and Benaiah the son of Jehoiada was over the Cherethites and the Pelethites; and the sons of David were chief about the king" (1 Chron. 18:14-17).

David had two supreme military officers, one to command forces in the field and the other, David's bodyguard, to keep order at home. He had two religious officers under Abiathar. He also had two civil officers, one to keep him abreast of the business that needed to be done and the other to keep the public informed of what had been done. The people thus were made aware of any new laws and kept in personal touch with the king. It worked well The people loved him.

It is the leader's job to keep a well-balanced program underway It is so easy for him to promote one aspect of the job at the expense of another. He can get a fund drive going and neglect evangelism. He can have a strong evangelistic thrust and neglect the training of his people. He can be so concerned about the organizational aspect and administrative details that he loses sight of the broad objectives. Imbalance usually comes when the leader allows himself to focus on work that he enjoys while avoiding the attendant responsibilities that are a part of the job. The ability to take the bitter with the sweet is one of the marks of a good leader.

Personal Problems: Sorrow and Affliction

A leader is not exempt from the personal problems of life. Financial difficulties may plague him. He may face severe testings with his children. Sickness in the family may bring a burden tough to cope with. He may face personal attacks on his motives or character or integrity. The storms of life may rage around him and appear at times to overwhelm him in their fury. Heartache, concern, and perplexity are not strangers to the man in a position of leadership.

The Apostle Paul talked about this: "And not only so, but we glory in tribulation also: knowing that tribulation worketh patience; and patience, experience; and experience, hope; and hope maketh not ashamed; because the love of God is shed abroad in our hearts by the Holy Ghost which is given unto us" (Rom. 5:3-5) When I read that passage I am struck with the fact that the apostle says we glory or rejoice in tribulation. Why? What's so neat about tribulation? Why would a perfectly normal, sane person glory in it? To most of us, tribulation is to be avoided, but here it is presented as something to be gloried in. This is a strange paradox for tribulation surely means pressure, affliction, and trouble.

The word rendered *tribulation* here comes from a term for an ancient threshing instrument by which wheat was separated from chaff. This gives us a clue as to why Paul gloried in it. And not only Paul. Other New Testament writers bring out the same idea

Peter wrote, "Behold, think it not strange concerning the fiery trial which is to try you, as though some strange thing happened unto you" (1 Peter 4:12). James tells us, "My brethren, count it all joy when ye fall into divers temptations; knowing this, that the trying of your faith worketh patience. But let patience have her perfect work, that ye may be perfect and entire, wanting nothing" (James 1:2-4).

Amazing! My natural tendency is to count it all joy when I climb *out of* divers temptations, not when I fall into them!

The Apostle Paul told the Colossians to respond to extended suffering with joyfulness and thanksgiving! "Strengthened with all might, according to His glorious power, unto all patience and longsuffering with *joyfulness; giving thanks* unto the Father, which hath made us meet to be partakers of the inheritance of the saints in light" (Col. 1:11-12).

As we read these passages we can see why trials and troubles are to be welcomed with thanksgiving and joy. It is through them that God builds Christian character. Endurance and staying power are produced in our lives. We must not lose sight of God's way of doing things. Endurance is a basic quality essential to leadership, and this is God's method of making it a part of us. A tree raised in a hot house is perfectly healthy but is tall and spindly. A tree that grows where the wind blows hard sinks its roots down deep. It is rugged, strong, and has staying power. That's what the leader needs. When trials come, they strengthen our faith, and the experience produces confidence in God for the future.

Paul writes, "And He said unto me, 'My grace is sufficient for thee: for My strength is made perfect in weakness.' Most gladly therefore will I rather glory in my infirmities, that the power of Christ may rest upon me. Therefore I take pleasure in infirmities, in reproaches, in necessities, in persecutions, in distresses for Christ's sake: for when I am weak, then am I strong" (2 Cor. 12:9-10). We must face the fact that God is more concerned with our completeness (maturity) than our comfort. It is His desire that the many facets of the beauty of Christ may shine through our lives.

Have you ever visited a pottery factory? When the pottery is placed in the kiln, its colors are dull and muted. After it has been in the fire—when it comes out of the oven—its colors are vivid. The fire makes it beautiful. So it is in our lives. The fires of life bring out the beauty of the life of Christ within.

Lila Trotman, the wife of the founder of The Navigators, has faced many a storm. But when Lila walks into a room, the place lights up. She radiates a beauty and freshness of spirit that is a wonder to behold. The beauty of Christ shines through.

This only happens, of course, when we face the tribulations of life in the light of the cross of Christ. Otherwise adversity can drive a wedge between us and the Lord. We may become bitter. So we must face up to our troubles and trust God to use them to accomplish His purposes and to do His work in us.

In addition to manifesting the beauty of Christ, tribulations can be used to demonstrate the power of God. Paul and Silas had been beaten, thrown into prison, and put in the stocks. In spite of the fact that their civil rights had been violated and they were treated unlawfully, what do we find them doing? Singing! Protest songs? No! They are singing songs of praise to God.

Paul practiced in Philippi what he preached in his letter to the Colossians. When they suffered long they were to respond with thanksgiving and joy. This would be a manifestation of the almighty, glorious power of God at work in them. "Strengthened with all might, according to His glorious power, unto all patience and long-suffering with joyfulness" (Col. 1:11).

There is a great deal of discussion concerning how the power of God is manifested in a life. Paul tells us that when a person is going through the flames of adversity with the spirit of joy and thanksgiving, that's power.

And, as Moses turned aside to observe the bush that burned but was not consumed, so people are challenged by the life that comes through the fires singing the praises of God.

One of the most helpful Scriptures to keep in mind during difficult days is given to us by Isaiah: " 'For My thoughts are not your thoughts, neither are your ways My ways,' saith the Lord. 'For as the heavens are higher than the earth, so are My ways higher than your ways, and My thoughts than your thoughts' " (Isa. 55:8-9). As we pray for deliverance we must keep in mind that God has His own timetable and ways. This is illustrated clearly in the experience of the Apostle Paul. At Antioch of Pisidia he was thrown out of town (Acts 13:50). He went from there to Iconium, where they tried to stone him, but he escaped (Acts 14:5-6). He fled next to Lystra, where he was stoned and left for dead (Acts 14:19). That's two escapes out of three possible assaults, which isn't bad according to the law of averages, though a person can hardly afford even one miss of this magnitude, since it's likely to be fatal!

In recounting this tale Paul, however, makes an astounding statement, "But thou hast fully known my doctrine, manner of life, purpose, faith, longsuffering, charity, patience, persecutions, afflictions, which came unto me at Antioch, at Iconium, at Lystra; what persecutions I endured: but out of them all the Lord delivered me" (2 Tim. 3:10-11). Did Paul really mean "*out* of them *all*"? At Antioch, yes; at Iconium, yes; but at Lystra he was stoned and left for dead.

Still Paul says he was delivered out of them all, and herein lies a beautiful truth. Paul was delivered twice *from* the stones and once *through* them! But in each case it was the deliverance of God. Paul would, no doubt, have chosen to be delivered from them in *each* case, but God's ways are not always ours. Paul came through these experiences with a glowing testimony to the delivering and preserving power of God. "And the Lord shall deliver me from every evil work and will preserve me unto His heavenly kingdom: to whom be glory for ever and ever. Amen" (2 Tim. 4:18).

"We know that all things work together for good to them that love God, to them who are the called according to His purpose" (Rom. 8:28). The truth of this statement is easy to understand but it's hard to live out in daily life. When the leader is in the midst of the furnace of affliction it is tough to have that assurance.

While I am writing this, my wife is making an apple pie. If she were to offer me a handful of vegetable shortening to eat for lunch, I'd say, "No thanks." The same would be true if she offered me a cup of flour or some baking powder. I'd explain to her that I'm not all that wild about baking powder, flour, and shortening. But when she puts these ingredients in the mixing bowl with others, works them all together, and places the mixture in the heat of the oven for a while, then it is a different story.

That's what God often does with our lives. He works together a blend of good times and tough times, and He knows the exact mixture that is good for us. We go through the fires of tribulation, and when the process is complete we are better people for it. The secret is to realize what God is doing and "glory in tribulations," to respond with thanksgiving and joy.

So, when you find yourself troubled or perplexed or persecuted or cast down, rejoice! God is building endurance and hope "that ye may be perfect and entire, wanting nothing" (James 1:4). And, if you are facing these things now, cheer up! You're in mighty good company. Paul wrote, "We are troubled on every side, yet not distressed; we are perplexed, but not in despair; persecuted, but not forsaken; cast down, but not destroyed" (2 Cor. 4:8-9). In addition to that, Paul was constantly facing death. "For we which live are always delivered unto death for Jesus' sake, that the life also of Jesus might be made manifest in our mortal flesh" (2 Cor. 4:11).

What kept Paul going in the face of all this? He lists five things. The first was faith. "We having the same spirit of faith, according as it is written, 'I believed, and therefore have I spoken.' We also believe, and therefore speak" (2 Cor. 4:13). The second was hope. "Knowing that He which raised up the Lord Jesus shall raise up us also by Jesus, and shall present us with you" (2 Cor. 4:14). Third was the needs of others. "For whether we be beside ourselves, it is to God: or whether we be sober, it is for your cause" (2 Cor. 5:13). Fourth was the benefit of his own soul. "For which cause we faint not; but though our outward man perish, yet the inward man is renewed day by day" (2 Cor. 4:16). Fifth was the fact that he viewed everything in the light of eternity. "For our light affliction, which is but for a moment, worketh for us a far more exceeding and eternal weight of glory; while we look not at the things which are seen, but at the things which are not seen: for the things which are seen are temporal; but the things which are not seen are eternal" (2 Cor. 4:17-18).

If we can keep things in perspective, present suffering which seems heavy and long is really light and short. But we must face adversity in the light of the cross and the perspective of heaven and remember it is working for our good—not against us.

What are some practical steps the leader can take when he is in the midst of trouble and sorrow? First of all he can take Scripture seriously. "Casting all your care upon Him; for He careth for you" (1 Peter 5:7).

I had memorized this verse as a new Christian, but it wasn't until recently that the full truth of it became part of my experience. I was talking with Dr. Bill Bright of Campus Crusade for Christ, sharing with him some of the heartaches and difficulties I was experiencing.

He looked at me and said, "LeRoy, I have found great comfort in 1 Peter 5:7." He went on, "I have concluded in my own life that either I carry my burdens or Jesus does. We cannot both carry them and I've decided to cast them on Him."

He challenged me to try it. I left that motel room bewildered. Did that verse actually mean what it said? I went to my room and began to pray. To the best of my ability I did what Bill had said. For months I had carried a heavy knot in my stomach. I could actually feel the thing leaving. I experienced the deliverance of God. No, the problem did not go away, and hasn't to this day. But the burden is gone. I no longer spend sleepless nights or cry myself to sleep. I can honestly face the burdens with a joyful spirit and thankfulness of heart.

During their journeys, the children of Israel "came to Marah, [and] they could not drink of the waters of Marah, for they were bitter" (Ex. 15:23). This was followed by Elim, where they found sweet water and fruitful palms. "And they came to Elim, where were 12 wells of water, and 70 palm trees: and they encamped there by the waters" (Ex. 15:27).

I know that in my own life, the bitter waters of Marah have been followed by sweeter fellowship with my Lord and greater fruitfulness in His service.

10

Surviving Dangers

Rattlesnakes are fairly common where I live. I encounter one almost every summer. It is a frightening experience to see a rattlesnake coiled, looking at you, ready to strike. He's lightning quick and accurate. I have a two-point program for rattlesnakes: shun and avoid. You don't need much insight to figure out what to do with something as dangerous as an old diamondback rattler. You don't mess around.

A friend of mine tried to pick up a rattlesnake once. He wound up in the hospital. It didn't kill him—got him with one fang only—but Bob was a mighty sick young man. His finger—where it bit him—is all shriveled up today. One advantage in dealing with these snakes is they don't try to trick you. When they shake their rattles and show you their fangs, you know what you are up against.

Unfortunately that's not so with many of the dangers that can kill off a leader. All too often these menaces appear to be harmless or masquerade behind a cloak of respectability. Some, on the other hand, come right out in the open and leave you with no doubt in your mind. They show their fangs. You know where you stand. Let's look at some dangers to leadership.

Some years ago I was gathering some men around me to make a thrust for Christ among university students. Bob Stephens, a young Air Force officer who was separated from the service, wrote a letter to me expressing an interest in the program. I wrote back and told him I had a couple of questions I wanted to ask.

The first was: "Do you think we can involve fellows in this

ministry who hate God?" Bob is a brilliant young man, an honors graduate from the School of Engineering at the University of Maryland. It didn't take him long to figure out the answer. When he replied no, I sent him this Scripture: "No man can serve two masters: for either he will hate the one, and love the other; or else he will hold to the one, and despise the other. Ye cannot serve God and mammon" (Matt. 6:24).

With the verse I sent another question: "Do you think we can have men working with us who are enemies of the cross of Christ?" He said no, so I sent him another verse: "Brethren, be followers together of me, and mark them which walk so as ye have us for an example. For many walk, of whom I have told you often, and now tell you even weeping, that they are the enemies of the cross of Christ: whose end is destruction, whose god is their belly, and whose glory is in their shame, who mind earthly things" (Phil. 3:17-19).

In that passage Paul says that the enemies of the cross "mind earthly things." They are all wrapped up in the things of this world and as such are living exactly opposite to the spirit of the cross, which is one of self-sacrificing love.

Bob agreed. He came with a desire to give of himself. For 20 years he has served in that spirit. The sin of covetousness has never gripped his soul. God has used him greatly around the world. Young men on three continents trace their spiritual roots to the influence of Christ through Bob's life.

Covetousness

Covetousness is one of those sins totally repudiated by the Apostle Paul. "For neither at any time used we flattering words, as ye know, nor a cloke of covetousness; God is witness" (1 Thes. 2:5). Personal gain was not a motive that lurked in the shadows of his ministry. If it had, he would not have been used as he was in the ministry of planting thriving churches.

Furthermore, he would not have been practicing what he preached. He told the Colossians, "If ye then be risen with Christ, seek those things which are above, where Christ sitteth on the right hand of God. Set your affection on things above, not on things on the earth. . . . Mortify therefore your members which are upon the earth; fornication, uncleanness, inordinate affection, evil concupiscence, and covetousness, which is idolatry" (Col. 3:1-5). Note that covetousness is idolatry, and the Apostle John also writes, "Little children, keep yourselves from idols" (1 John 5:21).

Why is covetousness so deadly to the spiritual leader? For at least two reasons. One, covetousness makes the leader lose his perspective—his life becomes focused on *this* world. Jesus said, "My kingdom is not of this world" (John 18:36). If the leader is occupied with the things of this world, his mind is diverted into unprofitable pursuits. He is living for the temporal rather than the eternal.

Jesus lived and died to bring *eternal* life to the world. The leader therefore must not live to enhance his own circumstances with personal gain. Because of the subtlety of this danger he must constantly be on guard, heeding John's warning: "Love not the world, neither the things that are in the world. If any man love the world, the love of the Father is not in him. For all that is in the world, the lust of the flesh, and the lust of the eyes, and the pride of life, is not of the Father, but is of the world. And the world passeth away, and the lust thereof: but he that doeth the will of God abideth forever" (1 John 2:15-17).

I once heard an evangelist brag that he could preach for two weeks and never wear the same suit twice! The scandal of men who heap up treasure to themselves has been a blot on the ministry.

This is not to say that the work of Christ should not be well-financed. The New Testament notes that the apostles had ample funds. It was common for people to sell their possessions and goods for the advancement of the work. Barnabas, "having land, sold it, and brought the money, and laid it at the apostles' feet" (Acts 4:37). But the money did not go to enhance the apostles' personal fortunes. Peter said, "Silver and gold have I none" (Acts 3:6).

The second reason covetousness is so deadly is that when a person gives God second place, soon He has no place at all. Covetousness is an insidious sin that grows in the hidden places of the heart. God said, "Thou shalt have no other gods before Me" (Ex. 20:3). Idolatry is loving anything more than God. Today few gods are made of stone or tree stumps. Most of the gods of this world are composed of tinted glass, baked-on enamel, and chrome, or dacron and wool, or silk, or alligator leather.

I recall an incident with a young man who aspired to leadership in the cause of Christ. He and I were having a discussion at the Bible school from which he was to graduate that spring. He had done well academically and seemed to have great potential for

God. I asked him what he was going to do upon graduation. He grew reflective, and I could see that he was thinking deeply. I began to wonder what he was going to say. Did he aspire to be a missionary in some remote jungle? Would he risk his life to take the Gospel behind the iron curtain. My imagination ran wild.

Finally he looked up at me and in earnest and serious tones said, "I think I'll buy a Buick!"

My heart sank. I was dumbfounded! Here was a man with potential for God's service whose mind was taken up with the passing glitter of this life. The command of Paul had not sunk in enough to govern his inner motivation: "And be not conformed to this world, but be ye transformed by the renewing of your mind, that ye may prove what is that good, and acceptable, and perfect will of God" (Rom. 12:2). The love of Christ was not pressing in on him to impel him to higher and nobler goals (see 2 Cor. 5:14-15).

The issue, of course, is not whether we are rich or poor. Some of the wealthiest people I know are dedicated men and women of God, who occupy strategic places of leadership in the cause of Christ. Covetousness is a condition of the heart, not the pocketbook. The things of this life can be used for Christ. Possessions can be as slaves or masters. They can hold us or we can use them. The person who has wealth and uses it wisely can be a blessing to hundreds of people.

People who are caught in the grip of covetousness are pitiful to behold. Satisfaction eludes them—all the way to the grave. "He that loveth silver shall not be satisfied with silver; nor he that loveth abundance with increase: this is also vanity" (Ecc. 5:10).

Paul warns two classes of people. The first are those who live *to get rich.* "But they that *will be rich* fall into temptation and a snare, and into many foolish and hurtful lusts, which drown men in destruction and perdition. For the love of money is the root of all evil: which while some coveted after, they have erred from the faith, and pierced themselves through with many sorrows" (1 Tim. 6:9-10).

Such a snare is a very real threat. It struck close to Paul himself when Demas forsook Paul, "having loved this present world" (2 Tim. 4:10). Though he was a companion of the great apostle, Demas failed to heed this warning. It was his undoing.

The second group warned *are those who are rich.* "Charge them that are rich in this world, that they be not highminded, nor trust in uncertain riches, but in the living God, who giveth us all things richly to enjoy; that they do good, that they be rich in good works, ready to distribute, willing to communicate; laying up in store for themselves a good foundation against the time to come, that they may lay hold on eternal life" (1 Tim. 6:17-19). The rich are tempted to pride, to trust in the wealth of this world and not in God. They must live with eternity in mind, and use their wealth accordingly.

Jesus spoke on this topic as well. A man, thinking himself wronged by his brother, came to Jesus and said, "Master, speak to my brother, that he divide the inheritance with me." Jesus answered, "Man, who made Me a judge or a divider over you?" Then He addressed the watching multitude, "Take heed and beware of covetousness: for a man's life consisteth not in the abundance of the things which he possesseth" (Luke 12:13-15). He did not sympathize with the man who claimed he was being cheated by his brother. He tried to raise everyone there from the sin of covetousness. One man had the money and the other wanted it. They were both in the clutches of covetousness. Jesus then told a parable that describes as a fool the man who "layeth up treasure for himself and is not rich toward God."

The leader will do well to search his heart on this matter to make certain he is not sliding into the subtle and deadly trap.

Self-glory

The second deadly danger to the leader is pride. Paul wrote, "Nor of men sought we glory, neither of you, nor yet of others" (1 Thes. 2:6). He had just repudiated the sin of covetousness (v. 5). Now he does the same with self-glory, the seeking of honor and prestige.

Here is another subtle trap. It happens so naturally that often one does not realize it. If you are a speaker at a conference or leading a group, things can take place to make you stand out as a very special person. It's happened to me: "There goes LeRoy Eims. He's leading one of the workshops at the conference" / "LeRoy, come over and chat for a minute. I have some friends who have been wanting to meet you" / "Leroy, join us on the platform tonight, greet the congregation and lead us in prayer" / "LeRoy, come join us at a special luncheon today. It's much quieter and more comfortable than eating in the dining room with the regular conferees."

Recently I was at a conference where some of these things

were happening. I was falling into the trap of enjoying it and feeling important. I was having a quiet time on the second day, and the Holy Spirit spoke to me very directly and personally from the Word of God. I was reading in Mark and these verses stood out like a neon light: "And He said unto them in His doctrine, 'Beware of the scribes, which love to go in long clothing, and love salutations in the marketplaces, and the chief seats in the synagogues, and the uppermost rooms at feasts; which devour widows' houses, and for a pretense make long prayers: these shall receive greater damnation" (Mark 12:38-40).

The Lord said in effect, "Do you love all these things that are happening, that make you feel important?"

"Yes, Lord."

"Do you love the salutation of people who feed your ego?"

"Yes, Lord."

"Do you love going up on the platform and being seen with all those important people?"

"Yes, Lord."

I reread the passage a number of times, then went to my knees, confessed my sins, and got right with the Lord. I sensed His comfort and forgiveness. Thank God for His promise: "If we confess our sins, He is faithful and just to forgive us our sins and to cleanse us from all unrighteousness" (1 John 1:9).

God's forgiveness was so complete that I found I could kid myself about the whole thing. It all seemed so empty and stupid once the Holy Spirit had brought it into the open. When I would enter the hall on the ensuing days of the conference, I would admonish myself, "OK dummy, don't act like a scribe." I'm sure many people who saw me wondered what I was smiling about. But I knew. I was amused by the foolishness and stupidity of seeking glory and was enjoying a renewed sense of closeness to God.

The leader will do well not to underestimate the danger of which the Apostle Paul warned when he wrote, "Let us not be desirous of vainglory." An incident in Paul's life illustrates his personal fear of the worship of men. Barnabas and Paul were being mightily used of God at Lystra. So much so that the people said, "The gods are come down to us in the likeness of men" (Acts 14:11). When the apostles realized that the people intended to offer sacrifices to them as gods, "they rent their clothes, and ran in among the people, crying out, and saying, 'Sirs, why do ye these things? We also are men of like passions with you, and preach unto you that ye should turn from these vanities unto the living God' " (Acts 14:14-15).

Actually, the apostles faced *two* dangers at Lystra. One was the worship and praise of men. The second was the wrath and persecution of the same people. "And there came thither certain Jews from Antioch and Iconium, who persuaded the people, and having stoned Paul, drew him out of the city, supposing he had been dead" (Acts 14:19). By far, the greatest of these dangers was the first. The apostles did not rend their garments when the people spoke of stoning them. They did, however, when the people wanted to worship them. Paul and Barnabas feared the worship of men more than their persecution, and rightly so.

Recently I heard a Christian leader tell of the subtleties of pride in his own life. When the mission director came with the missionary's immediate supervisor to visit him at his station he would put on an air of super-spirituality. He might have been sitting around reading a newsmagazine, but when his leaders came he would hide the magazines and pretend to be reading his Bible. He practiced this deceit in order to get a good report card. He wanted them to leave his area singing his praises. But Scripture says we are to minister "not with eye service as men-pleasers; but as the servants of Christ, doing the will of God from the heart" (Eph. 6:6).

People seem especially vulnerable to the sin of seeking to glorify self in three areas, each involving something commendable and good in itself. The first is in our giving. A pastor may seek to impress others in his denomination with the size of the missionary budget of his church. A Sunday School teacher can try to outdo other classes in the church so that it will go on the records and be seen by all. An individual can give generously to certain causes so that his name will appear on a special list or so that some leader might find out about it and drop him a personal note.

Jesus said, "Take heed that ye do not your alms before men, to be seen of them: otherwise ye have no reward of your Father which is in heaven. Therefore when thou doest thine alms, do not sound a trumpet before thee, as the hypocrites do in the synagogues and in the streets, that they may have glory of men. Verily I say unto you, they have their reward. But when thou doest alms, let not thy left hand know what thy right hand doeth: that thine alms may be in secret: and thy Father which seeth in secret Himself shall reward thee openly" (Matt. 6:1-4).

The second area in which the leader must guard his motives is in his production for the Lord. Annual denominational reports that tell of the successes of certain pastors in "adding to the flock" can be deadly. The pastor who is doing well can find himself hoping that "Mr. Big" will see the statistics and be impressed. Remember two things in this. First, it is the Lord who adds to the church. "And the Lord added to the church daily such as should be saved" (Acts 2:47). Second, pride may lead to a fall. David got caught up in the sin of numbering the people, and that which he thought would bring him joy brought him heartache. "So the Lord sent pestilence upon Israel: And there fell of Israel 70,000 men" (1 Chron. 21:14).

The Lord has sent us forth as laborers, and as such He expects us to do what we can to further the message that will bring people into the kingdom. And the more the better. God is pleased when our labors are used by the Spirit of God to populate heaven and add to the number of disciples. But let's make sure we do it "as to the Lord and not unto men."

The third danger area for pride is in our service for Christ. Paul speaks of "serving the Lord with all humility of mind" (Acts 20:19). He was serving God, not men. It is easy to slip into the sin of doing our best when someone important is watching and will commend us, but to let things slide when just ordinary folks are around.

My wife is a constant challenge to me in this regard. The way she sets the table is a classic example. She does it the same way for family as she does for company. Occasionally we will have a missionary or a Christian leader in for dinner. She puts on no airs on their behalf. Whether guests are present or not, there is always a centerpiece. Peanut butter, jelly, jam, pickles, mustard, catsup, olives, relish—anything she serves is always presented tastefully in a serving dish rather than from the jar or bottle. Milk does not come to the table in a carton. The table never looks like a junkyard filled with jars, boxes, and bottles. The napkins and silverware are placed properly whether for company or just family. She never just "throws it on." She keeps house as unto the Lord and tries to do her best for Him at all times (not as a pattern for others, but as a personal conviction).

Discouragement
The third deadly danger to the leader is discouragement. The

devil is a master at causing this. Far too many leaders have been driven from their works in the depths of despair. Things haven't gone right, plans have fallen apart, critics have constantly reminded them of their shortcomings. People they thought they could count on either didn't carry their load or turned against them.

How does a leader handle this problem? We all face it. No one is immune. It's rather surprising to see the record of Scripture concerning men of God caught up in the web of discouragement.

In Elijah's case, discouragement followed a great victory. That, by the way, is a rather common occurrence. A triumph is often followed by an emotional letdown or discouragement of some kind. Elijah had just prevailed spectacularly over the prophets of Baal on Mount Carmel. Baal's prophets had prayed, gashed themselves with knives, and cried out all day, but to no avail. They got no answers; their altar remained unlit. Then Elijah prayed a mighty prayer of faith, and God answered in such an unmistakable, fiery way that the people fell on their faces and said, "The Lord, He is the God" (1 Kings 18:39).

Then things started to fall apart. Jezebel, the queen, heard what had happened. She sent a message to Elijah saying she was going to kill him. Having a woman mad at you can be discouraging, especially if she is evil and powerful like Jezebel. Elijah fled for his life.

Four lessons emerge from the results of discouragement in this story. First, discouragement brings a false sense of values. "But he himself went a day's journey into the wilderness, and came and sat down under a juniper tree; and he requested for himself that he might die, and said, 'It is enough; now, O Lord, take away my life; for I am not better than my fathers' " (1 Kings 19:4). What Elijah said in effect was, "We've all got to die sometime, so why not now. I am no different from anyone else and since I'm going to die eventually, why not now?" But he was wrong. Elijah did not die—ever—for God had other plans for him. Years later, in God's time, "there appeared a chariot of fire, and horses of fire, and parted them both asunder; and Elijah went up by a whirlwind into heaven" (2 Kings 2:11).

Second, discouragement can cause us to run from our responsibilities. "And he came thither unto a cave, and lodged there; and behold, the word of the Lord came to him, and He said unto him, 'What doest thou here, Elijah?' " (1 Kings 19:9) The leader can begin to look around and conclude that the grass is greener on the other side of the fence. He can give up the work that God has assigned him. If he gives up or runs out on people who are looking to him for leadership, God is likely to come to him and say, "What are you doing here? Your place is in the job I gave you."

Third, discouragement can cause a person to begin to blame others for his predicament. He can start pointing his finger at people around him and denounce them for his troubles. "And he said, 'I have been very jealous for the Lord God of hosts: for the children of Israel have forsaken Thy covenant, thrown down Thine altars, and slain Thy prophets with the sword; and I, even I only, am left; and they seek my life, to take it away' " (1 Kings 19:10). It's all their fault.

Fourth, discouragement can cause the leader to blow things completely out of perspective. Elijah cried out that he was the only man in the whole realm who had remained faithful to God. But the Lord said, "Not quite." He stated, "Yet I have left Me 7,000 in Israel, all the knees which have not bowed unto Baal, and every mouth which has not kissed him" (1 Kings 19:18). Things were dark and bleak for Elijah as he looked at them through the situation as he saw it. But the facts were completely different. Things were actually 7,000 times better than he thought.

Most of us can testify to the reality of that experience. When we are in the midst of a problem, nothing seems to turn out right. But things are rarely what they seem during those bleak days. When the fog lifts and the storm clears, we see a bit more clearly and things are often about 7,000 times better than they appeared.

David had a similar experience. He had left his city unprotected and when he returned it had been burned and the women and children taken captive (1 Sam. 30:3). The reaction of David and his men was normal: "Then David and the people that were with him lifted up their voices and wept, until they had no more power to weep" (1 Sam. 30:4). So here we find David caught up in sorrow and despair.

At that point an almost unbelievable thing happened. David's men, his comrades-in-arms, men who had followed him through thick and thin, spoke of stoning him. The one thing that David had always been able to rely on when everything else fell apart was the loyalty of these men. On more than one occasion they had risked their lives for him. That which he knew he could count on was no longer there. He was alone.

This forced David to turn to the one Person who was always near. He "encouraged himself in the Lord his God" (1 Sam. 30:6). The Lord told him to pursue his ancient enemy and the final outcome was beautiful. David recovered all that the Amalekites had carried away. "And there was nothing lacking to them, neither small nor great, neither sons nor daughters, neither spoil, nor anything that they had taken to them. David recovered all" (1 Sam. 30:19).

In spite of the fact that things had never looked worse, the facts were that things were never better. Their wives and children were unhurt. His city had been burned, but *he was not going to need it anymore.* His kingdom was being prepared for him. Saul had died in battle, and David was about to be ushered into the palace. When things looked their worst, had they known the facts they would have been rejoicing. They would have sung praises to God rather than lifting up their voices and weeping "until they had no more power to weep."

Discouragement often has that effect. Problems can be blown completely out of perspective. Molehills become mountains. The leader must continue to walk by faith and wait till the picture clears. The Apostle Paul is a pacesetter in this. His arrival in Philippi had been followed by trouble and discouragement. But as he looked back he was able to say, "But I would that ye should understand, brethren, that the things which happened unto me have fallen out rather unto the furtherance of the Gospel" (Phil. 1:12).

Three things then can be the downfall of a leader: A covetous heart, a craving for self-glory, or discouragement. The enemy of our souls has been using these in the lives of men since Adam fell. There is no human defense against them. Satan knows how to circumvent, sweep aside, and destroy our human defenses.

But God wants to deliver us, and will if we trust Him. As an old man, David could look back over his years of experience with God and say, "Thine, O Lord, is the greatness, and the power, and the glory, and the victory, and the majesty: for all that is in the heaven and in the earth is Thine; Thine is the Kingdom, O Lord, and Thou art exalted as head above all. . . . Now therefore, our God, we thank Thee, and praise Thy glorious name" (1 Chron. 29:11-13).

11

Meeting the Needs
of the Group

One of the prime goals of a Christian leader should be the deepening of the spiritual lives of the people he leads. They must grow in grace and in the knowledge of Christ, developing in their effectiveness for Him and deepening in their devotion. It is God's desire that they demonstrate Christlike qualities in everyday life.

The Bible is alive with examples of this. Under David's leadership the men around him won battle after battle, defending the kingdom against the enemies of God. But the greatest accomplishments were in the lives of the men themselves.

How were these men described when they came to David? "And every one that was in distress, and every one that was in debt, and every one that was discontented, gathered themselves unto him; and he became a captain over them: and there were with him about 400 men" (1 Sam. 22:2).

Later, after lengthy association with David, these men became strong, dedicated, mighty men of valor. Scripture describes one of them, Eleazar, as "one of the three mighty men with David, when they defied the Philistines that were there gathered together to battle, and the men of Israel were gone away: He arose, and smote the Philistines until his hand was weary, and his hand clave unto the sword: and the Lord wrought a great victory that day; and the people returned after him only to spoil" (2 Sam. 23:9-10).

"It Takes One to Make One"

The influence of leaders on their associates is an interesting thing

116

to observe throughout the Bible. For instance, how many giant-killers were in Saul's army? None. When Goliath defied the armies of God, they quaked with fear (see 1 Sam. 17:11). David, who came to bring food to his brothers, sized up the situation, went out in faith, and killed the giant.

After David, the giant-killer, became king, how many giant-killers arose in Israel? Quite a few. They were almost a common commodity in the army under David's leadership. "Sibbechai the Hushathite slew Sippai, that was of the children of the giant . . . Elhanan the son of Jair slew Lahmi the brother of Goliath the Gittite, whose spear staff was like a weaver's beam. And yet again there was war at Gath, where was a man of great stature, whose fingers and toes were four and twenty, six on each hand, and six on each foot: and he also was the son of the giant. But when he defied Israel, Jonathan the son of Shimea David's brother slew him. These were born unto the giant in Gath; and they fell by the hand of David, and by the hand of his servants" (1 Chron. 20:4-8).

Why do you suppose there were no giant-killers in Saul's army? One reason, I'm sure, was because Saul himself was not one. However, under David's leadership they were numerous. Why? Because David was one. This illustrates a tremendous principle of leadership, a principle which runs throughout the Bible. *It takes one to make one.*

Our Lord's last command was "go, make disciples among all nations." Naturally, the command was not given to the multitudes but to the eleven men—his disciples. Why? *It takes one to make one.*

Therefore, if you are going to see strong, devoted disciples of Christ raised up under your leadership, you yourself must be one. *It takes one to make one.*

More on that later. But for now, let's ask how we go about this task. What can we do to see men and women of God raised up to serve Him?

It will become obvious to you as you lead that not all of the members of your group have the same devotion and desire to grow. Some are more eager and dedicated than others. This simple fact requires that you figure out a way to keep the interest and motivation of each person high and at the same time help those who are more on fire to develop to the maximum. Let us suggest a two-point program.

Voluntary Study Groups

First, arrange a special volunteer Bible study and prayer group. I have found this to be of tremendous value. Here are a few tips that may help you get a group started.

When you detect a special hunger and interest on the part of a few people, go to them privately and ask if they would be interested in meeting for Bible study and prayer at an early morning hour some day each week.

The advantages of meeting early in the morning are twofold. First, it avoids taking an evening. People don't generally need one more evening taken up with something. Quite often they are gone from their families too much already. Second, the early hour eliminates the half-hearted. Only the most dedicated will rise a couple hours early one day each week. After you have three or four people "signed up," announce this special Bible study and prayer time to the entire group. Invite anyone who wants to join you to do so. No one can then accuse you of playing favorites, of showing more interest in and giving more time to certain ones. Make your invitation "come one, come all—everybody welcome!"

As a matter of fact, you will probably be surprised at who comes. Often a deep fire burns in the soul of one who shows little outward evidence. Tell them that the rules and standards of the group will be decided on at a breakfast meeting the coming week. That's important. The specifics of how you spend your time should be discussed and decided together, within the framework of some working principles that you lay out for them in line with your objectives.

When you meet at breakfast to make plans, begin by telling them the purpose you have in mind. A few well-selected Scripture verses will help clarify some specific goals and give your presentation some punch and authority. A few passages that I have found helpful follow. I have shared various of these with different groups, depending on their level of maturity and depth of interests.

Romans 8:29: "For whom He did foreknow, He also did predestinate to be conformed to the image of His Son, that He might be the firstborn among many brethren." Goal: to become more like Jesus.

John 5:39: "Search the Scriptures; for in them ye think ye have eternal life: and they are they which testify of Me." Goal: to learn more about Jesus.

Acts 20:32: "And now, brethren, I commend you to God, and to the word of His grace, which is able to build you up, and to give you an inheritance among all them which are sanctified." Goal: to be built up in the Word of God.

Matthew 9:36-38: "But when He saw the multitudes, He was moved with compassion on them, because they fainted, and were scattered abroad, as sheep having no shepherd. Then saith He unto His disciples. 'The harvest truly is plenteous, but the laborers are few; Pray ye therefore the Lord of the harvest, that He will send forth laborers into His harvest.' " Goal: to spend time praying that God will raise up laborers for the harvest fields of the world.

Psalm 119:9, 11: "Wherewithal shall a young man cleanse his way? By taking heed thereto according to Thy Word. Thy Word have I hid in mine heart, that I might not sin against Thee." Goal: to memorize Scripture—for clean lives.

Psalm 119:105: "Thy Word is a lamp unto my feet, and a light unto my path." Goal: to apply the Scriptures as our light and lamp—for guidance.

Jeremiah 33:3: "Call unto Me, and I will answer thee, and shew thee great and mighty things, which thou knowest not." Goal: to pray for specific needs in our lives.

Hebrews 11:6: "But without faith it is impossible to please Him: for he that cometh to God must believe that He is, and that He is a rewarder of them that diligently seek Him." Goal: to deepen our faith.

Select a Bible study program for the group to use. One that has been used with great profit by groups around the world is "Design for Discipleship," a six-booklet Bible study program developed for either individual or group use. It can be ordered from The Navigators, P.O. Box 1659, Colorado Springs, Colo. 80901.

Many other excellent Bible study guides are available through your Christian bookstore. My own book, *Winning Ways,* could be used to study witnessing. *Disciples Are Made—Not Born* by Walt Henrichsen, *Know Why You Believe* and *Know What You Believe* by Paul Little, *What Did Jesus Say About That?* by Stanley C. Baldwin are all good, to name just a few.

Assign a chapter for discussion the following week. Have each person complete his study before coming to the study group. This insures a lively Bible-based discussion when you meet. You might want to make a phone call sometime during the week to each member of the group to see how they are coming on their study. A personal contact by phone and time spent in prayer for each of them will be used of God to stimulate faithfulness and desire on their part.

When you meet, allow adequate time for prayer. One early morning group that I led for a year had a strong personal witnessing outreach as one of its objectives. This prompted us to pray along the specific lines of evangelism. We based our prayer time on four passages of Scripture:

Colossians 4:2-4: "Continue in prayer, and watch in the same with thanksgiving; withal praying also for us, that God would open unto us a door of utterance, to speak the mystery of Christ, for which I am also in bonds: that I may make it manifest as I ought to speak." In this passage Paul prays for an open door to speak the mystery of Christ. In our group we made a list of people and began praying that God would open an opportunity to witness to them. We made these people specific subjects of personal daily prayer as well as praying for them together in the group.

Acts 16:14 speaks of Lydia "whose heart the Lord opened." We made a list of people to whom we had witnessed and who seemed to show some interest, and prayed that God would open their hearts.

Colossians 1:9-10: "For this cause we also, since the day we heard it, do not cease to pray for you, and to desire that ye might be filled with the knowledge of His will in all wisdom and spiritual understanding; that ye might walk worthy of the Lord unto all pleasing, being fruitful in every good work, and increasing in the knowledge of God." We made a list of each person who came to Christ through our witness and prayed for their growth and maturity in Christ.

Matthew 9:36-38: "But when He saw the multitudes, He was moved with compassion on them, because they fainted, and were scattered abroad, as sheep having no shepherd. Then saith He unto His disciples, 'The harvest truly is plenteous, but the laborers are few; pray ye therefore the Lord of the harvest, that He will send forth laborers into His harvest.'" We made no list from these verses but simply prayed that God would raise up laborers in our midst. I might add that three of the five members of that group are today serving the Lord as missionaries—in Argentina, Indonesia, and Lebanon.

If your group is highly motivated to learn the Word of God, a plan of Scripture memory can be incorporated. Decide how many Scripture verses you will memorize each week, and spend about five minutes of your time together in checking each other on your verses. The group can pair off by twos, each person quoting his verses to the other person. Memorize the reference with the verse and strive for word perfection. The Navigators' Topical Memory System has been used by Christians all over the world. It can be ordered from The Navigators.

Personal Time

The second part of your program to keep the highly-motivated growing toward spiritual maturity is similar to the first but more intense.

After you have had your study group for a few months, it will become evident to you that one or two members of the group are growing faster and showing greater spiritual hunger than the others. These are the ones you have been waiting for! God is preparing them for greater use in His kingdom. Go to these people personally and ask if they would like to meet on a personal basis—man to man—for some special training. Explain that you would like to have lunch with them to explain fully what you have in mind.

God has spoken to my own heart about this phase of leadership from Isaiah 58:10: "And if thou draw out thy soul to the hungry, and satisfy the afflicted soul; then shall thy light rise in obscurity, and thy darkness be as the noonday." When I observe a person who has a special hunger to learn the Scriptures and grow in grace, I must be willing to share my life with him and pass along those things that God has taught me.

Paul spoke of this also: "Ye are witnesses, and God also, how holily and justly and unblameably we behaved ourselves among you that believe: As ye know how we exhorted and comforted and charged every one of you, as a father doth his children" (1 Thes. 2:10-11).

Note the phrase "as a father doth his children." How does a father train his children? Always on an individual basis! My 23-year-old daughter has a completely different set of interests and needs from those of my 17-year-old son. I must make time for each of them individually to discuss the issues of life they are facing at the time.

The concept of the leader spending time individually with his key man is as old as the concept of leadership itself. Moses prayed that God would give him a man to be his successor. "And Moses spake unto the Lord, saying, 'Let the Lord, the God of the spirits of all flesh, set a man over the congregation, which may go out before them, . . . and which may lead them out, and which may bring them in; that the congregation of the Lord be not as sheep which have no shepherd' " (Num. 27:15-17).

Later the Lord instructed Moses: "But charge Joshua, and encourage him, and strengthen him: for he shall go over before this people, and he shall cause them to inherit the land which thou shalt see" (Deut. 3:28). Note that God assigned Moses the task of *charging, encouraging,* and *strengthening* Joshua. This was a man to man ministry.

As you compare this command to Moses with 1 Thessalonians 2:11 (*exhort, comfort, charge*) and 1 Corinthians 14:3 (*edify exhort, comfort*), an interesting pattern emerges. This gives us a great deal of guidance as to what to do with those with whom we will meet individually. I try to include four things during these times together.

1. Edification: share things with him that will edify and build him up in the faith. Make your training time a positive thing. Build upon his strengths. Encourage him to develop his gifts.

2. Exhortation: from time to time it is necessary to point out areas in the man's life that need to be brought back into line with the Word of God.

3. Comfort: help him with the things that are bugging him. Encourage him when he is down. Help him meet his problem.

4. Charge: assign him special projects that will help meet specific needs in his life or build on his gifts and abilities. Begin to familiarize yourself with devotional booklets and guides that you can give him to read and discuss with you later.

Through these special times with you the life of this person will be tremendously affected. But another thing will occur. Others in the group will notice his growth, greater dedication, and greater familiarity with the Scriptures. This will prompt a hunger on their part and a desire to experience the same thing.

Some years ago I had the responsibility of leading a Sunday evening church youth group. I began to share with them the principles of spiritual growth and Christian maturity.

After a couple of months, one young man named Jerry developed a real hunger for the things of God. He would corner me from time to time and ask questions that revealed a heart that was very tender toward the Lord.

I suggested we meet for special prayer and study on Sunday morning before Sunday School. He had a paper route and finished up about 8:30 in the morning, so that's when we met. I got him into personal Bible study and Scripture memory, and he began to have a daily quiet time with the Lord.

Jerry grew like a weed. Soon others in the class noticed this and began to inquire what was going on in Jerry's life. When we explained, others wanted to get in on it. Soon we had a hard core of kids who were showing many of the characteristics of true discipleship.

Jerry began to help another guy, and soon the process of multiplication was operating throughout the group. The idea is contained in 2 Timothy 2:2: "And the things that thou hast heard of me among many witnesses, the same commit thou to faithful men, who shall be able to teach others also." Paul to Timothy to faithful men to others also.

When I begin meeting with a man to train him in godly living and effective outreach, am I satisfied when he comes to me and tells me he has led someone to Christ?

No, I'm happy but not satisfied. I want him to not only be able to lead someone to Christ, but pass along to that person the principles of Christian growth.

When he begins to do that am I satisfied?

No, I'm happy but not satisfied. I want him to stick with his man until he in turn is used of God to lead another person to Christ.

Am I now satisfied?

No, I want that person in turn to be able to repeat the process with the new man.

Am I satisfied now? Yes, because that will be clear evidence to me that the man I helped originally has fully caught the idea.

Let me illustrate. Let's say I help Pete in his Christian life, and one day he leads Joe to Christ. I now know that Pete has been brought to the place of maturity where he can lead a person to Christ, but I still don't know whether he knows how to follow that person up.

It is not until Joe begins to mature and eventually leads someone to Christ that I know for sure that Pete knows how to train Joe to lead a person to Christ and follow him up to the point where he can go and do likewise. So it's when Joe comes to Pete and says, "I've led someone to Christ" that I know my training of Pete has been effective.

In this case it was LeRoy to Pete to Joe to Sam. So until I see Sam, I'm not sure that I'm really getting through to Pete. If you can grasp that idea it will make your leadership effective and productive beyond your wildest dreams. Meditate for a while on 2 Timothy 2:2. Ask God to multiply your life.

12

Communication

Communication is a vital part of leadership. The leader must frequently be in front of people. He may have to make announcements, teach lessons, introduce speakers, or give short talks. In one capacity or another he will be trying to get something across to others.

How do you get ready? What do you do to put your ideas together so that they make sense to your listeners? Are there any general rules to follow that will help you accomplish your objective? Let me begin by sharing a personal experience.

My wife and I were walking down the street of a small town in Iowa one Sunday morning some 20 years ago. I had a job with the railroad, which took me away from home frequently to various towns on the line, and Virginia had come to spend the weekend with me. We were at loose ends with nothing to do, and as we walked along we heard church bells.

Sort of as a joke I said, "Let's go to church."

She was a bit surprised and said, "What for?"

"Oh, I don't know," I answered, "lots of people do that sort of thing and we don't have anything to do 'til lunch time."

"OK," she said, "where shall we go?"

"I don't care. How about that one over there?" I pointed to one across the street.

So we went in and sat down. Naturally we felt a little out of place, but we settled down to see what would happen. We were in for the surprise of our lives. When the minister gave the sermon both of us became keenly interested. It wasn't his subject matter —though later we knew that he had preached the Gospel. What drew our interest was the *way* he did it. Two things stood out: you could tell that he knew what he was talking about, and he meant what he said.

Virginia and I had been to church before and had heard other preachers. But this was the first minister who had these two qualities. Some we had heard seemed to know what they were talking about, but spoke with no conviction—they didn't seem to mean it. Others meant what they said, but didn't seem to know what they were talking about.

Imperatives in Speaking

As I've reflected on that incident over the years, these two things have stood out more and more as vital in speaking.

First, *know your subject*. To establish confidence in the minds of your listeners, you must study and prepare carefully. Do your homework. If your audience realizes that you really have a grasp of your topic and that you are only sharing a part of all that you know, it gives them a sense of confidence and trust. They believe you.

Second, *say it like you mean it*. Naturally, the first leads into the second. You must be convinced in your own mind before others will be convinced. This is one of the things that made Jesus' ministry outstanding. It was said of Him that He spoke "as one having authority, and not as the scribes" (Matt. 7:29). The scribes were like schoolboys reciting a lesson; Jesus spoke with an authority and conviction that astounded His listeners.

Another incident in the New Testament bears witness to this truth. Paul and Barnabas, while ministering in Iconium, "went both together into the synagogue of the Jews, *and so spake,* that a great multitude both of the Jews and also of the Greeks believed" (Acts 14:1). "It is interesting to note how some of the newer versions and paraphrases render the phrase *and so spake:* "They spoke so effectively" (*New International Version*), "and spoke with such conviction" (*Phillips*), "and spoke so well" (*Berkeley*), "and spoke with such power" (*Amplified*).

Ponder those words *and so spake*. Frankly, I had read over that passage many times before I noticed the word *so*. And *so* spake! It was not only *what* they said; it was the way they said it.

The lesson is clear. The Holy Spirit is pointing out to us that

the *manner* with which we get our message across has something
to do with the reception it will get. A dull speaker, droning along
in a monotonous voice, soon has you feeling sleepy. Well, believe
me, the minister in that church some 20 years ago did not put me
to sleep. He held my attention. He knew what he was talking
about! And he meant what he said!

Content in Messages

OK, you say. I'm convinced. But how do I go about putting together a talk that is both interesting and accomplishes something?
As I have listened to speakers who communicate effectively, I
have learned two things.

First, *preach the Word*. By that I do not mean that you give a
Bible-based talk. More than that. Your talk must have Bible content. As you inject the Scriptures throughout, they give your message flavor and zest and power. The Holy Spirit takes His Sword
(see Eph. 6:17) to prick consciences and probe hearts. "For the
Word of God is quick, and powerful, and sharper than any two-
edged sword, piercing even to the dividing asunder of soul and
spirit, and of the joints and marrow, and is a discerner of the
thoughts and intents of the heart" (Heb. 4:12).

The Holy Spirit takes the Word and uses it to break down walls
of resistance to obedience and faith. " 'Is not My Word like as a
fire?' saith the Lord; 'and like a hammer that breaketh the rock
in pieces?' " (Jer. 23:29) So be sure to salt your talk generously
with the Word of God.

You learn the second important aspect of communication from
the life of Jesus: *tell stories*. Use illustrations. Jesus was the
master storyteller:

"No one ever spake like this man."

"Behold, a sower went forth to sow."

"A woman had a coin."

"A man had two sons."

"The kingdom of God is like . . . "

Use your illustration or story to help your audience understand
the point you are making and the Scripture you are using. Let
.ne demonstrate.

Recently I was asked to give a talk on how to get the Word of
God into our lives. One of the points I made was that we must learn
to meditate on the Scriptures: "O how I love Thy law! It is my
meditation all the day" (Ps. 119:97). I shared this illustration:

If you were to come to our home in the evening we would talk for awhile and then I might ask if you would like to see the rest of the house. As you started down to see the lower level, I could leave the lights off and hand you a birthday candle with which to look around. You would go from room to room and peer into the gloom, and soon you would return upstairs.

"What did you see?" I'd ask.

"Well, I saw a room with a Ping Pong table, a family room, a bedroom off the hall, and a room that looked like a small den or library."

"Right!" I'd say. "That's what's down there all right."

Then we would both go down, turn on all the lights, make ourselves comfortable, and look around the family room. Soon it would become apparent that a real decorator worked on this room. You'd notice the careful balance of colors and furnishings. You'd see how the pictures on the walls were just right and blended in well with the colors in the rug and furniture. Question: Did you see the family room with the birthday candle? Answer: Yes. But did you *really* see it as it is? No, you really saw it when we turned on all the lights, sat down, and took the time to let the beauty of the room come through.

This illustrates the difference between reading the Word and meditating on the Word. Often reading the Word can be like hurrying through the house with a birthday candle, glancing here and there, catching a glimpse of this and that. But the richness of the Word—its depth and beauty and wonder and majesty—only comes as we take the time to sit with it, ponder it in our minds, and let the Holy Spirit reveal its depths to us.

So then, here's the pattern:

1. State the point: Meditate on the Word.

2. State the Scripture: Psalm 119:97.

3. Give an illustration: The birthday candle story—to show the difference between reading and meditation.

If you have a talk that has three or four points, you repeat the process three or four times. After you give a brief introduction to your theme you make your points. For example:

How to Fill Our Lives with the Word
I. Study the Word
    A. Scripture—Proverbs 2:1-5; Acts 17:11
    B. Illustration—A man searching for treasure must dig deep;

      he rarely finds his precious metal lying around on top
      of the ground.

II. Memorize the Word
   A. Scripture—Colossians 3:16; Proverbs 7:1-3; Deuteron-
      omy 6:6-7.
   B. Illustration—The Vietnam prisoners-of-war who had
      memorized God's Word were able to use it to enable
      them to survive the rigors of the Hanoi Hilton and help
      other men as well.

III. Meditate on the Word
   A. Scripture—Psalm 119:97; Psalm 1:2-3; Joshua 1:8
   B. Illustration—The birthday candle story.

IV. Closing application
   Show a method of Scripture memory or Bible study they
   can use day by day on their own.

Notice that throughout the message the Scriptures are central.
A story or illustration adds a bit of spark and illumination. At the
end a practical application shows the group how to do something
about it. Try this approach each time you give a talk. Speakers
often challenge and exhort us, leaving us with the desire to follow
through. But they say nothing about *how* we could do it. A leader
must be practical and provide the "how-to."

When you use a story or illustration, be sure to select one to
which your audience can relate. A wheat farmer in Kansas would
see things differently from a factory worker in New Jersey. We
have not all bumped our heads on the same brick wall.

An illustration I once used in Singapore is a classic example
of how not to do it. In trying to make my point, I told a story of
two guys in Nevada who almost froze to death in a driving snowstorm. My audience had never heard of Nevada, had never seen
snow, and couldn't imagine anyone freezing to death. I would
have been far better off talking about the three Hebrew youths in
the burning, fiery furnace. Singapore, after all, *is* hot!

Overcoming Nervousness

A major obstacle to overcome in speaking is nervousness. I know
—I have this problem. In fact, whether I'm witnessing to one
person or speaking to a group, I find that my throat gets dry and
my hands get wet. I wish it were the other way around, but it never
is. A verse that comforts me in regard to this problem is: "But

sanctify the Lord God in your hearts: and be ready always to give an answer to every man that asketh you a reason of the hope that is in you with meekness and fear" (1 Peter 3:15).

Notice Peter says, "With meekness and fear." So if you feel a bit fearful, rejoice! You qualify! If God wanted us to be brash and to have the feeling we are well-qualified in our own intellect and strength, He would have said so. But when the butterflies begin to rise in our stomachs, our hands begin to shake, our knees begin to knock, and our throats get dry, that's when we find ourselves on our knees before God asking for His grace and strength. And that's when He can use us.

"And He said unto me, 'My grace is sufficient for thee, for My strength is made perfect in weakness.' Most gladly therefore will I rather glory in my infirmities, that the power of Christ may rest upon me. Therefore I take pleasure in infirmities, in reproaches, in necessities, in persecutions, in distresses for Christ's sake; for when I am weak, then am I strong" (2 Cor. 12:9-10).

Often I have to speak to an unfriendly audience. My talk might be in a college dorm or classroom or in a meeting in the student union. Usually some students come to the meeting to try to prove I am wrong, and who object to the message of the Gospel. I've learned a couple of things the hard way that help overcome nervousness.

First, when you are giving a message that sticks to the Word of God, you have an advantage that should give you the boldness of Daniel. That advantage is this: *what you are saying is true.* Whether people believe it or not doesn't change the fact. Jesus said, "Thy Word is truth" (John 17:17). Paul spoke of "the Word of the truth of the Gospel" (Col. 1:5). In a world where the only constant is change, it is a blessed thing to know that your message, the Word of God, is eternal Truth. "Being born again, not of corruptible seed, but of incorruptible, by the Word of God, which liveth and abideth for ever. For all flesh is as grass, and all the glory of man as the flower of grass. The grass withereth, and the flower thereof falleth away: But the Word of the Lord endureth for ever. And this is the Word which by the Gospel is preached unto you" (1 Peter 1:32-25).

Second, it helps to *smile.* The shortest distance between two people is a friendly smile. It sort of takes the edge off your nervousness and their hostility. As I said, this is one of those things I learned the hard way.

Lorne Sanny, Walt Henrichsen, and I were in the Pacific Northwest on a ministry trip. When we arrived at Oregon State University, I was amazed to see huge signs across the length of the high-rise dormitories reading, "LeRoy is coming." Immediately fear gripped me. I just knew that at our meeting that night a gang would be waiting to skin me alive. When LeRoy came, they'd be waiting.

The meeting was held in a large classroom and there was a good turnout. I arrived feeling nervous and apprehensive as to the outcome. The emcee got the meeting started and turned it over to me. I looked over the audience and noted what seemed to be a sinister pocket of bushy-haired radicals. So I grimly began my presentation—unsmiling—and laid it out hard and clear. To my amazement they listened with great interest, and when we opened up for questions theirs were honest and sincere.

After the meeting ended they came up to the front, shook hands and said, "Praise the Lord, Brother! It's sure great to hear the Gospel presented so clearly. Thank you for coming." For the first time all night I smiled.

On the way home Lorne said to me, "You should have smiled once in a while. It would have helped give the meeting a little warmth." I knew he was right and learned another valuable lesson.

The Major Ingredient
Prayer is an essential part of message preparation and presentation. Pray before you begin to prepare and pray before you make your presentation. Pray that the Holy Spirit will give you the right Scriptures and illustrations and that He will enable you to give the message under His power.

This was another one of those lessons I learned the hard way. For two years in the mid-50s I was on a team that presented the Gospel to fraternities and sororities at the University of Pittsburgh and at Carnegie Tech. We would go in on Monday evenings, present the Gospel, make appointments, and then talk to these individuals during the week.

One of the things we decided at the outset was to pray together before each meeting. We were working with Campus Crusade for Christ at the time, and Bill Bright of Crusade had urged us to spend much time on our knees with God before we went to each meeting. The Lord laid on our hearts the necessity of this prayer time, and we were faithful in it. The Lord blessed our efforts, and soon we had quite a large number of new converts whom we were leading in Bible study. Some of them in turn were going to other fraternities and giving their testimonies as part of our team. Things were going well.

I suppose we became complacent or proud or overconfident or something, but our prayer time began to grow lax. Then one night it happened. I was busy and the rest of the team had things to do, so we met at the fraternity house where we were to speak, out of breath and in a rush. One of us offered a hasty sentence prayer, and we hurried into the meeting.

I could tell from the moment the meeting started it was going to be a disaster. The emcee couldn't get proper attention. The men who gave their testimonies sounded like robots giving a stock market report. When I stood up to speak, there was absolutely no sense of the presence of the Holy Spirit ministering to hearts. It was a canned speech and nothing more. When we closed the meeting they politely hustled us out of the house.

We looked at each other and knew what we had to do. We got into our car and spent a good deal of time in prayer, confessing our sin to God and asking His forgiveness. That was the last time we neglected our prayer time before the meeting. The Lord heard our prayers and continued to bless His Word. And through it all we learned a lesson we'll never forget.

"Not that we are sufficient of ourselves to think any thing as of ourselves; but our sufficiency is of God; who also hath made us able ministers of the new testament; not of the letter, but of the spirit: for the letter killeth, but the spirit giveth life" (2 Cor. 3:5-6). "I can do all things through Christ which strengtheneth me" (Phil. 4:13).

OTHER BOOKS BY LEROY EIMS

BE A MOTIVATIONAL LEADER LeRoy Eims shows how to maintain high motivation and morale within a group, equipping people to be and do their best for Christ. For church, home, business, and community leaders. Textbook **6-1008**/Leader's Guide (with transparency masters) **6-1808.**

WINNING WAYS Suggestions, by LeRoy Eims, on how to prepare for witnessing, approaches that can lead to witnessing, and how to witness so that people will listen. Textbook **6-2707**/Leader's Guide **6-2921.**

WHAT EVERY CHRISTIAN SHOULD KNOW ABOUT GROWING LeRoy Eims displays a contagious sincerity and love for the Lord as he leads new believers into patterns of healthy Christian growth and discipleship. Textbook **6-2727**/ Leader's Guide **6-2947.**